Healthy LITTLE EATERS

Healthy LITTLE EATERS

How to help your children develop a healthy relationship with food

WAL HERRING

RANDOM HOUSE
NEW ZEALAND

CONTENTS

PART II – FOUNDATIONS

PART III – LET'S GET DIRTY

PART IV – ONWARDS AND UPWARDS

ACKNOWLEDGEMENTS

First I would like to thank my parents, Hilda and Toot Doel. What amazing parents! You instilled many beliefs in my subconscious while I was growing up, including two that I know directly helped me write this book: everything needs to be practical; and when something is not working there is always room to look at it differently and find another solution. Without these beliefs this book would never have eventuated.

Ben, my supportive yet challenging husband. I love the way you care as much for my dreams as you do for your own, and that you challenge me to not just talk big but to follow it through. This book would still be an idea in my head if you had not said, 'Stop the talking about this book. Pick a date and get it to me.' Thank you.

My three beautiful children. Some believe that children pick their parents. If this is so, I am thankful every day that you picked me to be your mum. I watch you grow and try to teach you the best way I can, yet on some days I cannot help but think you are teaching me more than I am teaching you. This book would never be what it is without you three in my life.

Thanks to all my friends, family, clients and blog-readers for your support in answering my many questions about what makes a healthy relationship with food. Also for all the support and feedback I received that helped to make this book what it is today. A special mention to Haidee Stradford for being a part of the virtual brainstorming effort — you nailed the title.

Rachael Taylor, Associate Professor at the University of Otago, I greatly appreciate you taking time to read this book and write the foreword.

Last but not least, publisher Margaret Sinclair, project editor Tessa

King, designer Kate Barraclough and the team at Penguin Random House. I am continually astounded at the effort and work you put into this book. It is a slick-run operation but has felt very personalised every step of the way. I am truly grateful.

FOREWORD

We currently live in a world that encourages us to overeat and puts us at risk of ill health — both physically and mentally. Food advertising is ubiquitous, and it's generally not for foods that should form the bulk of our diets. Many people do not have the ability or sometimes the knowledge to grow and prepare their own food from scratch. Our children learn from a young age that food and situations are closely linked; that lollies might be offered when they hurt themselves for example, and that dessert follows vegetables. Yet research tells us that many of the food-related practices we use as parents might not actually be doing what we intended. There is no doubt that all parents want the best for their children, and to have a happy home life. Yet battles around food are commonplace and can be exhausting. Encouraging children to eat healthily and have a good attitude to food seems relatively straightforward in theory, but why do so many of us find it difficult in practice? Food is tied into our emotional psyche very closely —in ways we might not understand. As this book describes, we often parent as we were parented. Sometimes this is great, and sometimes there might just be an even better way. This book will both challenge and inspire you to think a little differently about how you interact with your child around food. It provides anecdotes, ideas, and most importantly solutions for *how* to encourage your children to develop a life-long love of 'good' food — the food that is going to make them feel good and enjoy life.

Rachael Taylor
Research Associate Professor
Karitane Fellow in Early Childhood Obesity
Edgar Diabetes and Obesity Research
University of Otago
November 2015

PREFACE

I care. I care about you. I care that you struggle at dinner times with your children. I care that you don't look forward to it; maybe even resent the fact you have to slave over dinner, putting effort into cooking a healthy meal only for your children to reject it. I care that you feel that your children seem to be the only ones who won't eat vegetables. I care that they go sweet-crazy when they're out. I care that you are judging yourself based on what your children do.

There is more. There is a better way. I want to show it to you.

This book will show you a different approach to mealtimes, a different approach to life. The outcome is twofold: firstly, it will help you to have happier, more peaceful mealtimes, with you having increased confidence in your parenting; and secondly, it will help your children grow up with an unconscious positive association with food, a healthy relationship with it.

So many people have emotional attachments to food. They battle food, sneak food, feel guilty over what they eat, and often eat out of boredom. They think that they should eat this and shouldn't eat that, a constant internal battle. This is an energy drainer. It doesn't have to be this way.

As parents we are constantly searching for ways to parent our children better than we currently know how to. I know you can raise kids who eat food because they love it and choose food that makes them feel good. In this book I will show you how.

Teaching your children to have a healthy relationship with food will impact on your life and the lives of your children in ways that you may never fully appreciate. It will become your and your children's personal belief and habit.

All the information I will present in this book is common practice in some households, even in some cultures as a whole, yet the people who have children who seem to eat everything don't know what they are doing, and those who struggle with their children don't know why they struggle. There are little bits of information everywhere, but you have to go searching for it. This is where this book comes in.

Health, nutrition and changing lifestyles for the better are passions of mine. I get excited about them. I get excited about helping people to make long-lasting changes to their diet. I have a huge smile as I write this. I cannot explain the feeling I get just thinking about reading and researching about how to take my health to the next level, and how to then teach this to others and see the benefits they will receive. This is the time when I feel most alive.

My background is varied. Growing up on a farm in a small community in the north of New Zealand taught me that theories about life are one thing, but being practical is another. I spent five years at the University of Otago, obtaining a Master of Science in Nutrition and a Bachelor of Physical Education. During this time I had treatment for Hodgkin's disease (a type of lymphatic cancer). This experience taught me that if you want something enough, there are no excuses.

I have travelled the world and lived in England, Japan and Canada, and currently reside in the south of New Zealand. Experiencing different communities and cultures has taught me that everyone is different.

I have three children. Parenting has been a great gift, yet at times I have felt extremely personally challenged by it. I have often questioned if I am doing 'the right thing'.

Living in different countries and communities, having children and consistently reflecting on how I can be a better nutritionist and mother, I have come to realise that advocating one-size-fits-all solutions for nutrition or other lifestyle changes is not only impractical but often brings unnecessary stress.

This book is my gift to you. I have read and researched countless views and research about how to get children to want to eat healthy food now and in the future, both when we (parents) are around them and when they are away from us. I have observed and experimented on my own children. I have observed my husband and countless families at mealtimes. I have pondered how the information I have learnt could be passed on in an easy-to-implement manner. My hope is that our generation of parents will raise their children to have no 'food issues'; that our children will have a healthy relationship with food. This book is the start of you empowering your kids to have a positive experience with food.

When my children are disappointed by not knowing something, or when they try to do something but realise it is difficult, I always say, 'You don't know what you haven't learnt'. When reading this book, I hope you have many 'aha' moments. These may be closely followed by thinking 'what have I been doing to my children?'. It is super-easy to get down on yourself. After all, although you might not admit it, you want to be that elusive parent who gets everything right; that perfect parent with perfect children. My advice is to go easy on yourself: you don't know what you haven't learnt.

Even after reading this book, it will take time to change your habits. It is like learning anything in life; the more you do it, the better you become.

I truly care about you. I have written this book for you. It is my gift to you.

There is a better way. I wish you all the best in helping to raise children with a life-long healthy relationship with food.

INTRODUCTION

The main aim in parenting is to raise healthy children who know how to make wise decisions for themselves.

It is easy to get focused on getting our kids to eat that one piece of broccoli. But how will this teach them to choose good foods when they are not with you?

I know you want the best for your children. You provide your children with good food. You may make sure their protein, calcium and iron requirements are taken care of. You may go to great lengths to find out what they like to eat and provide them with food you know they will like, just so they eat something.

You give them food you know is good for them. Sometimes they eat it without question; others, mealtimes are like a battleground, a standoff. You may be happy because you know they are getting healthy food at home, yet you worry about them making the same 'right' choices when you are not with them. It can even be an area of contention between you and their grandparents or your children's friends' parents, who seem to feed your children all kinds of junk food — food you do not approve of, but that your children devour given the chance. Let's take a step back. What exactly do you want for your children by providing them with healthy food? My guess is that your response is the same as most parents': you want healthy children. Normal? Yes, but children are only children for a short time. You can only influence or control what your children eat for a short time.

Suppose you prepare the majority of their food for the first 20 of their 80 years (25 per cent of their lives). Even then, they will still make food choices away from you. This means you will dictate less than 25 per cent of their food choices in their lifetime. Becoming aware of this, you need to move the emphasis away from focusing on specific moments of nutrition — that one piece of broccoli — and on to shaping your children's long-term choices and habits. It needs to move from dictating, controlling and forcing children to eat healthily to teaching and coaching them to eat healthily throughout their lives.

The common mentality is to think about what you are giving to your children. Does it have enough protein for growth or calcium for strong bones? We then make food choices based on these 'requirements'. We justify that pizza is good because it has some tomatoes in the sauce and some protein and calcium in the cheese. We buy juice because it is a way to get fruit into children. It is how marketers get us to buy their food — it is fortified with vitamin D, calcium, etc. We make our children's food choices based on what we think is good for them. It is how our parents taught us. It is what most parents do, so we do it without questioning it. But what if this is short-term thinking? After all, we will only do this for less than 25 per cent of their lives; otherwise it is up to them to make the choices.

I grew up on a farm. We didn't have much money to buy those treats that other children had — at least, that is what I thought as a child. I now know it wasn't because we were worse off financially than those other children, it was because my parents had different priorities. Spending money on junk food was not a priority for them. Still, like many parents, they used bribery, rewards and guilt to get us to eat our vegetables. Although they were a little less strict on me than on my older sisters, when I left home I would not *choose* to eat a salad. In my mind it was something you did because you *should*.

When I left home, I was in control. I got to choose which foods I did and didn't eat. I went through a few too many years of eating food that I 'shouldn't' and not eating food that I 'should'. I came around though, and after a while I began not only preparing, but loving all sorts of vegetables and healthy food.

When I became a parent I assumed that this would be the path for my children. I would provide mostly healthy food, they would rebel when they left the house, but eventually they would come around to eating healthy again. 'What if they don't?' was a question that nagged me during dinner times which were not peaceful and repeatedly came down to a battle of wills. I realised how draining mealtimes were and I searched for answers.

Although I don't like to admit it now, I started on this path not because I wanted my children to have a healthy relationship with food, but because I was tired of fighting with them at mealtimes. I was tired of putting effort into cooking and being met with 'Ugh, I don't like this', before they even tried it. I was tired of being a grumpy mum. I was ashamed that my children were the ones going crazy for sweets at other people's houses. I was ashamed of the way they seemed to devour chips and lollies without even chewing.

I started to look into what affected children's food choices, in the present and in the future. I asked myself, 'How can I increase the possibility that my children will choose and want to eat healthy food when they leave our home? How can I teach them to have a healthy relationship with food?' I was faced with other questions: Do children need to go through a rebellious stage? Can parents coach their children to have a healthy relationship with food? One where children *want* to eat healthy and choose food that makes them feel awesome, where they don't use food as a reward, where they don't feel guilty eating food they know they 'shouldn't', where food is a non-issue? This started shaping what I believe is a healthy relationship with food.

WHAT IS HEALTHY EATING?

Healthy little children: we all want them. And how do you get healthy little children? By them eating healthy food, of course.

But have you stopped to ask yourself what healthy eating involves? When I ask my clients, they respond with something like 'eating fruit and vegetables'. Yes, that may be healthy eating but it is only half the equation. If your kids are eating healthy food only through your using control, guilt and restrictions — is this really healthy eating? I don't think so.

Healthy eating involves choosing and eating healthy food because you enjoy eating it *and* because it makes you feel so awesome! Healthy eating is about fostering a healthy relationship with food. Healthy eating is choosing to have an amazing salad because it energises you. Healthy eating is when you can have one piece of chocolate cake and not feel guilty about it, or not feel that you are being 'good' for not eating the whole thing.

Healthy eating is about eating food that nourishes you, physically and mentally. You can teach this to your children.

WE HAVE GONE ABOUT IT WRONG

Teaching healthy eating is not so much about concentrating on the what, but on the *how*. How can we teach our children to make healthy choices, because they *want* to, because ultimately it feels ten times better to have a diet filled with healthy food than it does to have a diet filled with processed food? When you focus on the how more than the what, the process becomes easier. It becomes about *coaching* children to develop food habits that will be the foundation of their lifetime, as opposed to enforcing rules — rules that they will probably break when they are not with you (or even if they continue to uphold these rules away from you, they do so with guilt and feelings of restriction and animosity).

How can you teach them to form a healthy relationship with food? Teaching your children to form a healthy relationship with food is like teaching them a new skill. And learning a new skill is like building a road. Literally.

Our brains are malleable. Think of brain connections like you would a highway. When babies first learn to walk, the neural connections are not formed. They first need to learn, among other things, to balance. Fast forward a few years and you can walk huge distances without actively thinking about how you need to balance on your feet. You do it automatically. You have these 'roads' in your head that you built over years of practice that allow these connections to flow easily. You practised walking so many times that now your brain takes over without a lot of active input on your part. You made a highway in your head, a highway of neural connections.

And to do it, you had to experience walking yourself. If you sat in a chair for the first 10 years of your life while someone explained how to walk in every detail, you would still not form these neural connections in your brain. When you tried to walk, you would still have to go through the slow process of building these neural roads through practice. The more you practise walking, the better and faster your 'road' becomes, until you are running, jumping, leaping and even flipping. No matter how much instruction you got on how to walk, you could not form the brain connections until you experienced it yourself.

Teaching children about healthy eating is like this. When parents take over, dictate and control their children's food intake, children do not make neural connections. They do not learn to make good decisions for themselves. They will make decisions based on external cues, such as emotions and advertising. They either slowly work out how to choose better food themselves or they never really learn how to choose food based on internal cues. Nutrition becomes about willpower and ultimately an internal battle.

Parenting is about helping your children build these roads, letting them experience the building of them. It's about asking them how they can do it better, guiding them to make choices. Parenting is giving them the resources and the know-how to build a road, yet standing back enough so they can figure out their own way. This gives your children the opportunity to not only experience life but to be empowered to do it in a way that suits them.

Teaching your children how to be responsible for themselves gives them the opportunity to possibly do things better than we currently know how to. Food will change, just as it has changed dramatically over the past 100 years, but the foundations stay the same. If you lay the foundation of healthy eating habits, the foods can change, yet your children will continue to make choices that ultimately will make them feel awesome — all because you taught them healthy habits that formed a healthy relationship with food.

As parents, we only have a short amount of time to teach our children. Teaching them how to make healthy choices for themselves and guiding them along this path will teach them healthy eating habits that will last a lifetime.

ABOUT THIS BOOK

This book is arranged in 12 chapters, progressing from your own awareness of food and defining what a healthy relationship with food means, to the foundations of encouraging your children to have a healthy relationship, to real, practical applications you can use.

Throughout the book, I have also included action steps. I encourage you to keep a journal to document the process of going through each step. As with the example of learning to walk, you can learn all the theory you like, but putting it into action is where brain connections are built and where you will ultimately see results.

PART I

Setting the Scene

CHAPTER ONE

YOU DON'T KNOW WHAT YOU DON'T KNOW

It all starts with you, literally. You decide what food your children are exposed to by what food you bring into your home, by what you eat and how you cook. You also influence what your children like by what foods you think your children should or should not like, ultimately affecting how many times you expose them to different foods.

Ninety-five per cent of our choices are subconscious — they are habits that we don't question.[1] Without you realising it, your own habits are influencing what foods your children are exposed to and how they are exposed to food. This shapes your children's eating. How you think and feel about food, and how you serve food, affects what your children will grow up to believe about food. You are a role model and children learn through osmosis, a process of absorption. Yet while a lot of people accept this fact, it can be hard to make the connections in our own lives.

When I was in my early twenties, at university, I witnessed a food-modelling experience that has stayed with me. I was 'sitting in' on the sessions of a registered nutritionist, who was consulting with a young girl, Susie,[2] and her mother Amanda. Susie was seven years old but weighed less than a three-year-old. A very loving mother, Amanda was naturally concerned and didn't know what to do. She was worried that her daughter was not eating enough, that she wasn't growing properly. She worried that Susie would go through the same things she herself went through as a teen.

Amanda spoke about how she had battled anorexia when she was just a little older than her daughter. She spoke about the pain of being hospitalised. She was fed through a tube to keep her alive and fought with food and her body image for her entire teenage years.

Although she was now in her forties, the pain and suffering she had experienced was still evident in her words and body language. While she said that her body-image issues were in the past and that she was okay now, the feeling I got was very different.

Although unable to fully comprehend it, Susie could see it, too. Amanda was Susie's role model. How Amanda acted and reacted around food was teaching Susie how she should react around food. When Amanda commented on her daughter's weight, saying 'Oh, look at how thin you are', Susie would reply, 'No, I'm not, you are', with a smirk on her face and a glimmer in her eyes. Susie was not eating and only pretending she was, because that was what she knew. Her mother was very thin and that was what Susie wanted for herself. Being stick-thin was like a badge of honour for Susie, because she wanted to be like her mother.

Children, especially in their early years, just want to be like adults and therefore look for role models — often their mother if they are girls, or their father if they are boys. They see and absorb everything. Amanda could not see that her food and body issues were shaping her daughter to have the same experiences. It was easier for her to pretend these issues were not there, or that it was a problem she needed to fix in her daughter, rather than face herself.

NOT ON THE SAME WAVELENGTH

Our brain emits electromagnetic fields, which allow scientists to measure these brainwave patterns through electroencephalography (ECG). Brainwave frequencies measured and recorded in adults range from low frequencies where the brain is not very active, as in deep sleep, to higher frequencies where the brain is very active, such as when we are wide awake and thinking. Babies and children have different brain frequencies during the different stages of their development.[3]

Between birth and two years of age, brain wavelengths are in the lowest range of frequencies, known as delta waves. As adults we experience delta frequencies when we are in a deep sleep. This means that babies see the outside world without analysis, judgement, editing or critical thinking. Experiences like the hotness of a fire (or getting burnt) are downloaded into the subconscious mind and beliefs and habits are formed (fires are hot and dangerous).

As an example, when my daughter Huxley was 16 months old she was getting confident climbing on playgrounds and going down slides. However, she once fell going down a slide and came down head-first, giving herself (and me) a terrible shock and receiving a good bump to the head. From then on she was timid of every and all slides. Huxley was about three and a half when she first started to go down a slide by herself again — and that was only after huge encouragement from both my husband (Ben) and me.

Some toddlers learn that slides are fun and you have to drag them away kicking and screaming because they want to do it 'one last time' (for the twentieth time), yet Huxley had an experience which taught her that slides were dangerous. Although by the time she was two she would not have remembered her fall, she had formed a subconscious pattern 'road' telling her that slides were dangerous and likely to cause pain.

Between two and five years of age, brain frequencies come up a notch and reach what scientists call theta waves. As adults we experience theta waves when we are in deep meditation or light sleep. Our brains are not asleep yet we are not fully awake and making judgements of what is real or not. If you have ever been hypnotised, you would have experienced being alert in a theta state. I recently saw a show in which the participants were told that the number seven did not exist. They struggled to count the fingers on their hands: although they knew they had 10 fingers, they would always count 11 because seven was missing from their consciousness!

Between the ages of five and eight children experience what scientists call alpha frequencies. Alpha frequencies are experienced in adults as a relaxed mental state — we are awake yet our eyes are most probably closed and we are relaxed. Daydreaming or light meditation are ways in which adults usually experience alpha frequencies. At this frequency children are still forming a good part of their subconscious minds — they do not yet have the ability to be analytical about their surroundings. This is why if you ask a child aged around six who has had no previous teaching about money if they would like to have two 50 cent coins or one $2 coin, they will choose the two 50 cents. They cannot yet conceive that one coin may be worth more than two coins.

After the alpha stage, children's brains start to move up into beta frequencies. This is when the analytical mind starts to form and draw conclusions about external life. As adults, we are most likely to be operating at this frequency at this moment, reading this book, as our brains are receiving and processing information. Therefore, when children are between zero and seven years old, their brains are like sponges. Their brains are more open and receptive to suggestions and messages during this period than they are at any other time of their lives.

Operating at this lower brain wavelength is ultimately a survival mechanism. A lowered brain wavelength helps small children to download information into their subconscious, making some actions become automatic. This mechanism helps to keep children safe by enabling them to learn the rules of the world and the society they live in.

MIRRORING YOU

Children's brains are not only in a state of high receptivity; they also contain a significant number of a certain type of neuron called a mirror neuron. Neurons are the basic building blocks of the nervous system and mirror neurons live up to their name: they help the child to mimic the behaviours they experience in the world. To experience mirror neurons in action, stick your tongue out at a baby. Their mirror neurons will fire and they will stick out their tongue right back.

Mirror neurons help babies to draw conclusions about the world around them — again, ultimately useful for our survival. Imagine an infant growing up in the wild. When a tiger approaches, the baby learns that tigers are dangerous by the way their parent acts. Young children do not need to get mauled in order to learn that tigers are dangerous; they learn through the reactions of the parents and adults around them, thanks to mirror neurons.

At times of uncertainty, babies read their parents' or a familiar adult's reactions from gestures, facial expressions and emotional reactions. You may have experienced seeing your first precious child fall over and get a bump. Your natural reaction is to rush to them with an expression of concern and worry. Your first child will learn that when they fall over and get a bump (no matter if it hurt or not), they should be concerned and may cry. By the time you have your third or fourth child you have come to realise that children and babies are much more resilient than you thought the first time around. When your youngest falls over, your reaction is less concerned and worried. They see this and, in turn, do not become overly concerned when they fall over again. Youngest children can usually take bigger knocks without crying or fussing.

Beliefs are not formed out of conscious thought — they are formed by watching and mirroring our parents and interpreting that information. Rasmus, my son, has always loved to run fast. When he was two, he would run around and around the kitchen island saying, 'Was that fast, Mum?' There was one catch: he did it naked. Before he ran fast he had to take his clothes off. When I asked him why, he would just look at me with an expression that said 'What do you mean?', then say, 'I need to run fast.'

The catalyst for my two-year-old son running around naked was my husband, who had taken him to his gym. Ben had taken off his shirt to work out. Although nothing was ever said, my son interpreted this simple action as 'you need to take off all your clothes if you want to run fast and be like daddy'. Once this was implanted in his brain, he never questioned it. It became part of Rasmus' two-year-old identity — to have no or limited clothes on when he ran.

The maxim 'Give me a child until he is seven and I will show you the man' was around well before we discovered the information about brainwaves and mirror neurons that you have been reading, but it hits the nail on the head. Children's brains up until about seven or eight years of age are in a state where they are forming their subconscious minds not only through their own experiences, but also from observing their parents and familiar adults' reactions to life experiences. Beliefs are formed, without critical thinking, and these form the basis of their adult belief system. These beliefs then form habits and ways of reacting to situations that are not questioned but are subconscious reactions.

We operate 95 per cent of the time from our subconscious patterns. The majority of this subconscious was formed during the time when we had no critical thinking or analytical abilities. On top of that, some of what we 'downloaded' into our subconscious was based on the reactions of our parents or familiar adults.

This can be a very confronting concept to take in and it could leave you feeling very overwhelmed. Yet that is only a reaction you have learnt!

While scientists once thought that our brains were fixed and non-changeable, we know that this is not true. We can learn new things or relearn a different reaction, and that includes the way we react to experiences.

I have learnt to view the fact we operate 95 per cent of the time based on things we learnt when we were children as very empowering, for two reasons. Firstly, you have been through this. You formed some of your current beliefs about food without thinking critically or any editing of information. You absorbed messages not only from the way your parents spoke but also from the way they interacted with food when you were young and you continue to not only believe this, but also have made them your habitual responses. When you identify some of those beliefs that may not serve you (this book will begin to help with this), they cease to control you. It's like going from walking around a dark room trying to get out and not knowing which way to go, to turning the lights on. You can see where the door is, you can see a way out. Rather than just reacting to circumstances, you can choose to respond or not to respond.

Secondly, your children are learning by osmosis or unconscious learning. Children do not take notes of what it means to be an adult and how they 'should' behave — they absorb this information through observation. They observe you as an adult — the mighty power. They absorb everything you do as a parent, good or bad. They pick up on how you respond to situations and this gives them cues about how they should behave. And it is not just what you say but also how you react to and interact with food.

Your beliefs about food and what food means to you as a parent stem from a variety of experiences that you have had over a lifetime and are unique to you. A large chunk of these were formed in your childhood years. You have probably never questioned them. Your subconscious or subtle belief about food then either directly or indirectly influences your choice of food, and the way you parent.

I remember the first time I started cooking bacon and eggs without some sort of toast. When I grew up, my parents cooked bacon and eggs, sometimes with beans, but always with toast. It was a habit and belief that I had, because my mother and her mother before her cooked bacon and eggs on toast. A few years ago, I wanted to cut down on my bread intake to try to improve my energy levels (and it did!), so I stopped having toast with my bacon and eggs, instead having broccoli or avocado. It was weird the first few times. I kept thinking something was missing! It was a belief that I grew up with that toast came with a cooked breakfast. However, I have gone without toast with my bacon and eggs for so many years that now it feels weird to have toast with a cooked breakfast!

YOUR VIEWS BECOME THEIRS

That four-year-old just ate a whole tomato! I am not talking about cut up, in a salad or even on toast. I am talking about a whole tomato, eaten as most would eat an apple.

I was doing that whole comparison thing — you know the one. None of us like to admit it, but we do it anyway. After seeing other children in our local playgroup or at friends' houses, we compare them with our children's behaviour or milestones. Sometimes this is expressed out loud: 'That child is not even out of nappies' — sometimes internally: 'Yep, my child is the best.' Admit it, we have all done it.

On this particular day I became aware of my unconscious food beliefs, just because a four-year-old ate a whole tomato.

If this situation had occurred a few years previously, before I had started thinking about the information presented here in *Healthy Little Eaters*, I would have chalked up this tomato eating as not normal, keeping me in my comfort zone. I would not have become aware of how what I thought affected what my children chose to eat. However, on this day I admitted that I had limited beliefs that were affecting what my children ate.

I started to think: Why do I think children would not like to eat tomatoes? Why do I think I should cut up tomatoes in order for my children to eat them?

I came up with all sorts of reasons, from Ben not liking tomatoes, to thinking tomatoes were one of those foods you introduce at a 'later stage' due to potential allergic reactions. What I quickly realised was that none of these answers got me close to the real issue.

Even if it was in a 'healthy' way, I thought that certain foods were for children and certain food were for adults. I reflected on how I would only give my children certain vegetables because they were the ones I had liked in my childhood. They were the ones I was given, the more 'kid-friendly' vegetables. I realised that I was limiting what food I was serving my children because of what I believed children liked. I realised that I had been serving food in a very limited way, because I didn't know any other way.

Ben and I lived in Japan for a couple of years when Huxley, our eldest daughter, was very young. In Japan, before you eat large grapes, it is common to peel off the skin. I watched on many occasions when some Japanese mum would stare, eyes like lily pads, as my daughter ate grapes with the skin on! Occasionally they would gently make a fuss, taking the grape from her and peeling it before giving it back to her. It is a belief and a common practice to peel a grape before you eat it. It is just what you do in Japan. When they saw my daughter eating a grape with the skin on they assumed that we had never had grapes before and offered to teach us how to eat them. I grew up eating grapes straight off the vine in my grandmother's back yard. I even ate so many on one occasion that I vomited grape skins, yet it never occurred to me to peel the skin off!

Just as I thought you needed to cut up a tomato to eat it, my Japanese friends thought you needed to peel a grape to eat it. You eat and serve certain foods the way you do because that is the only way you know how.

Becoming aware of your food beliefs is the first step. Everyone has different beliefs about food. Some beliefs you may be conscious of, such as whether or not you find peas tasty. Some beliefs you may not be conscious of, like my thinking you could not eat a tomato whole. Not strictly true or untrue, just a simple belief.

Beliefs are part of how you see the world or how you identify yourself in the world. Your children pick up on all these beliefs and they become a part of how they see the world, how they identify with the world. You shape your children's beliefs by what you believe.

I thought I knew everything when it came to what was healthy for my family. I thought creating healthy children was more about the what — *what* I fed my children on a day-to-day basis. When I started to read, research and do little experiments on my children, I came to the realisation that although what I served my children was important, *how* I served them was arguably more important. My subtle beliefs about food, those I had formed through observations in my childhood, were shaping how my children viewed and reacted to food.

IGNORANCE IS LIMITING

Food is a huge part of everyone's life. We cannot escape it: we need food to survive. We begin learning about food from an early age, from direct experiences of what our parents serve us, from how food is eaten (chopsticks, with fingers or a fork), to what constitutes a snack food. We also learn from indirect experiences how we should behave around food, what adults eat and what children eat, the expectations our parents have at dinner times, even if it is okay to go hungry. What we learn is not necessarily true, they are just beliefs.

We will now examine your beliefs around food, but before we do I just want to tell you a personal story. It is a story about how well-meaning adults wanted the best for me. They were concerned for me because of their own issues, and consequently instilled fears in me that something was wrong with me.

I developed bulimia when I was young. My seven-year battle started not because I was overweight, but because adults expected something to be wrong with me. This is a weird concept, I know, but follow me on this.

I was very fit and lean as a kid. I swam competitively and I loved to run. In fact, I don't think I walked many places. I was the 'why walk when you can run' child. Being the third child of three I had to keep up and I did everything as fast as I could. I was the child whose stomach muscles were noticeable even when wearing a full bathing suit.

I don't remember food being an issue. I ate meals with my family and snacked when I got hungry. Being so active I rarely thought about what I ate. That was until a well-meaning swimming coach took me aside and questioned me about my eating. I remember the very caring coach sitting me down and trying to get me to 'open up' about food and my body. The basic feeling I walked away with was that I was too thin and something must have been wrong with me to be that way.

The day my coach sat me down was the day my innocence around food changed. I developed a belief that something was wrong with me, that I must have an issue with food, because it wasn't normal to be as lean as I was without having some sort of problem.

I thought about this a lot. I started to look at other children's bodies, at what was 'normal'. I saw that my body was not 'normal'. I was skinnier and leaner than the rest. I started throwing up my meals — not because I was trying to be thin, but because I thought I needed a way to justify why I was so lean. Adults were trying to be well-meaning, but they interpreted my body weight through their eyes and their issues.

You can see a lot more and you will parent differently when you cease to parent based on your current beliefs. When we try seeing the world through our children's eyes, when we appreciate what drives them to eat certain foods, teaching them to develop a healthy relationship with food becomes easier. When you realise that your beliefs about food are not necessarily right or wrong, you can step back and choose what beliefs and habits you want to instil in your children. This is an extremely powerful position to be in as an adult. However, it is easier to stay ignorant to our beliefs. This keeps us safe. It is said that 'ignorance is bliss'. Ignorance is not bliss, it is limiting. When we don't know our own ignorance, we cannot outgrow it. We cannot see that there is more to life than we can currently see.

When I was young I was ignorant to what my mum did all day — when I moved out and went flatting, I realised that the cup I left on the side table as I watched TV didn't magically disappear. I realised that the shower didn't stay clean, but instead got a pink slime on it after a while. I had once asked my mother, who did everything for us as well as help run our dairy farm, what she did all day. When she replied 'I tidy up after you kids', I admit that I was perhaps judgemental of her, as I didn't appreciate how much she did.

When I left home and lived with others for the first time, I realised how my mother kept the house going. When I became a mother myself I truly experienced how ignorant and judgemental I had been. I outgrew this belief about my mother and developed a deeper relationship with her. Ignorance was bliss, but it also limited my relationship with my mother.

Shedding light on how you see food and what your beliefs are will help you overcome them. You will get a deeper understanding about yourself and your beliefs around food. This will ultimately help you to parent your children, and help you influence your children to develop a better relationship with food.

YOUR BELIEFS WERE ALL TAUGHT

We hold some foods on a pedestal and other foods we eat because we think they are good for us rather than tasting terrific. We generally use 'treat food' such as sweets, cake and ice-cream as a way to reward children or as a form of providing excitement. Have you ever said 'Yeehah, you get spinach for dinner!' — not in a sarcastic voice, but because you actually meant it?

Here comes a point that will change the way you see food. Do you believe that 'treat food' such as cake, ice-cream and lollies are delicious because it is true or because you have been taught that? If you answered it is true for me, it may only be true for you because you were taught it when you were so young it became a part of your subconscious!

When I have introduced this concept to parents, I can see an 'aha' moment spread across their faces. One parent said 'So you're saying that my son only likes sweet food because I taught that to him?' Well, yes and no. He has formed a belief that sweet food is good and other food is not, from his parents' and other adult figures' indirect actions, gestures and reactions towards food, which have been reinforced by wider society. It is not a one-time lesson but an ongoing belief that he has formed through his experiences and others' reactions.

While we will go into more details of what we can do to change these beliefs later, for now I just want you to become aware of what your subconscious beliefs are and start to challenge their truth. I get excited when I think of society having an underlying belief that healthy food is exciting and cake is a food that you have to endure at birthday times!

KID-FRIENDLY FOOD

Dave, a colleague of mine and father of two, turned to me and said, 'You know, "kid food".' This was not the first time I had heard the phrase 'kid food', but Dave was explaining to me that when he was away with work (and because he does the majority of the cooking), his wife would eat the food she served to the children: 'kid food'. He joked that she may have scurvy. (All jokes aside, Dave's wife felt unhealthy eating the food she gave her children at every meal. How did she think they were feeling? They might not comprehend how they feel, yet they still feel it.)

I have thought about this a lot since then. What exactly is 'kid food' anyway? I inquired more about what he thought 'kid food' was. He was talking about the commonly accepted food marketed at children. The white, fried child-food such as chicken nuggets, chips, fish fingers, etc. Somewhere along the way we, as a society, have developed a belief that children do not like any food that has any amount of natural colour. You may or may not have this particular belief but you will have some belief of what food kids like more than others. Think quickly now — what foods do you think are 'kid-friendly food'?

I asked myself this question. I had not served my children the 'kid food' that Dave had served his children, but I had succumbed to labelling certain vegetables and other food as more 'kid friendly' than others. There is a common belief that children don't like healthy food, that they will only eat unhealthy food in the form of white grains or processed meats or anything that is sugar-laden or fried. I had felt that only certain vegetables like potatoes, carrots and cucumbers were 'kid food', yet blue cheese, olives, eggplant and other vegetables were not 'kid food'. I am sure you are nodding your head in agreement. You may differ from me and my thoughts about what specific foods are 'kid friendly', yet you will still have some underlying beliefs about what you classify as 'kid friendly' for your children.

What food do you label as 'kid food'? How is this affecting what you give your children or even what you try to give them?

When Eckhart, my youngest, was starting solids, she was very selective about what she liked to eat. I tried her on a variety of foods, yet she seemed to reject most foods, even banana, which most babies will eat. She also rejected pumpkin and sweet potato. Having an unconscious belief that babies like banana, I kept on trying. Having an unconscious belief that babies might not like pumpkin, I stopped serving it to her. I had wanted her to like all food, yet my beliefs dictated what I actually gave her. She started out rejecting both pumpkin and banana; however, my actions (giving her banana many times but not persisting with pumpkin) told her she should like banana but it was okay not to like pumpkin.

This was also highlighted to me as Eckhart grew up. Throughout her life my awareness has been open to my beliefs about food and I have challenged myself to not limit her to foods that I think she will like. For example, when Rasmus and Huxley were at the stage of preferring to eat anything off my plate rather than theirs, if I was eating a spicy curry, I would say something like 'No, you cannot have this, it's too spicy.' If they kept insisting on trying it, I would give it to them, but when they reacted to the spice I would have said something like 'See, too hot', with an added expression of 'yuck' on my face.

With Eckhart, however, I never once set her up to believe a food was going to be something she didn't like. When she expressed interest in eating something off my plate I let her try it, with a neutral expression on my face, and then asked her 'Yum?' To my surprise she always went back for more. She continues to love hot curries and will even share the hot, sour lemon drink I have each morning.

Your beliefs, what you believe is 'kid food', or what you believe babies should like, affects what you serve them, how you react to them expressing interest in that food, how you react once they have tried it and ultimately how frequently you expose them to certain foods. This then shapes their eating preferences.

THEY WON'T LIKE THAT

Do you have expectations that your kids will like certain foods and not others? Do you serve limited food to your children because you think they will not like other foods?

I have been observing how parents, grandparents and caregivers interact with their children at mealtimes for a long time. On one occasion at a gathering, all the food was put out: ham, salmon and a few salads. As I went about putting a little bit of everything on my children's plates, I was offered an apology from the host because there was nothing there that the children would like to eat. I was at a bit of a loss — there was a large variety there. I am guessing my host thought 'kid food' was white and fried and that the colourful 'real food' on the table was not classed as food that children would like. This comment was made in earshot of Huxley. I ignored it and continued to put a little bit of everything on the kids' plates — the same sort of food that they had tried many times before and had not only eaten but had come back for seconds.

I wasn't paying much attention to what my children ate that day as there was a large number of people and my children were eating with the other children. After an hour or so Huxley came and asked me for some food, because she was hungry. When I asked her if she had had much of the food I had given her, she replied that she had not eaten all that much because it wasn't made for children.

When we label food 'food that children won't like', they are more likely to not try it, or if they do try it, they have an expectation they won't like it. Although I will cover this more in chapter four, for now I would like you to think about what food you have labelled as 'kid food' and 'not kid food'. Do you see how your beliefs are limiting what you expose your children to? Do you see how you are teaching your children what food they should or should not like?

This idea of 'kid food' is often reinforced by media and other children, but it starts (or ends) with you. Give food a clean slate. To teach children to like broccoli, start with your thoughts. Do something radical and have an expectation that your children will like the taste of broccoli, or at least learn to like the taste, because they are children and they should like broccoli.

Brian Wansink, an American expert on eating habits,[4] and his colleagues designed a study to test the effect of expectations on how we experience food. They bought a couple of bottles of low-end wine and changed the label on one. All the study's diners got the same thing, but one read 'Californian wine' and the other read 'North Dakota wine'. (California is known for its wines while North Dakota is not. It would be like getting a pinot noir from Central Otago versus a pinot noir from Northland.) The researchers found that the people who got the wine with the Californian label on it rated it as a better wine than the people who got the wine with the North Dakota label. The diners who had expected a good wine felt they got just that, whereas the diners who expected to have a poorer-quality wine rated it as such. They were both the same wine, yet because it was expected that the wine that was labelled as being from California was going to taste good, they rated it better than the one with the label from North Dakota.

You create expectations about food for your children. If you create an expectation that some food is 'adult food' that it is too spicy or more for mature taste buds (like blue cheese) then children are likely to decide that they don't or won't like it. Imagine doing the opposite. Imagine setting up an expectation that children should like all food and if they don't they just need to develop a taste for it by trying it more times (more in chapter seven).

HOW, WHAT, WHEN

What we grow up eating is what we are likely to eat as adults. Unless you have consciously changed or have been exposed to situations and cultures where they do things differently, chances are you eat the same food as when you were a kid. If you serve your children sugar-covered Fruit Loops for breakfast, chances are they will develop a habit that a sweet cereal is what they eat for breakfast. They will grow up with the habit of having a sugar fix to start their day.

When we had porridge growing up, we sprinkled brown sugar on top. That was how porridge was served. To this day I like a sweet-tasting porridge, although now I will mash a banana into it rather than smother it with brown sugar. I got this habit from observing my parents. My mum came to stay recently and every morning I made porridge. I laughed when she sprinkled her porridge with brown sugar, not knowing I was having an 'aha' moment of 'that is where I get my sweet-tasting porridge belief from'. She turned to me and said that when she was little, porridge meant cream and brown sugar. She felt it was wrong not to have cream and brown sugar on her porridge. How my grandmother and quite possibly her mother before her served their porridge was a belief passed on through generations. I have a belief that porridge should be sweet, because that is what I was taught as a child. Yet, because I am aware of this I have the ability to choose something different for my children. Their porridge is made plain and they love it! When the cousins came to stay and one of them had honey on her porridge, Huxley turned to me, screwed up her face as if to say 'yuck', and said 'I don't like my porridge sweet.'

While I still find it difficult to have porridge without anything sweet on it, I have consciously taught my children to like porridge plain. I am teaching my children a different habit, one where they don't need to start their day with something sweet. This will be what they know, and when they are faced with people who put brown sugar or even honey on their porridge, they may try it, but ultimately they will probably reject this, simply because in their minds that is not how porridge is meant to taste.

Adding sweetness to porridge is just an example of how beliefs around food are formed. How you serve food will stick with your children. And you will serve certain food to your children because that is what you grew up with. When I thought about the food I serve my children I also started to think about the way I served it. I gave lots of vegetable sticks to my children. They liked the texture of rawness, they liked how they were not mixed together, and I liked how they ate them. I got obsessed with vegetable sticks, not only in terms of what type of vegetables I gave, but in the way I cut them up.

One afternoon I was looking around the cookware department in our local homeware store. I came across an apple corer and remembered how my daughter would eat apples at my sister's place because she cored the apple. I purchased the apple corer and over the next few days cut up the children's apples differently. Sometimes I served them whole, sometimes cored and then sliced horizontally, sometimes vertically. Our average apple consumption in the house increased after purchasing the apple corer. The children had a choice of how they wanted their apple cut up and it was a little excitement for them.

I then tried this for other vegetable and fruits, cutting carrots into circles or grating them. Then I tried different ways of cooking vegetables: steamed, roasted or grated beetroot, or broccoli sautéed with tamari and butter. I served food that my children had liked before but had got bored with, and I did this by cooking or preparing it in different ways. Guess what happened? They liked the change and ate more of this food! They also got to choose which way they could have their carrots: raw — grated, stick or rounds; or cooked — roasted, steamed or sautéed. Part of getting kids to eat more good food starts with their autonomy and letting them make choices, which we go into more in chapter nine.

I remember the first time I cooked a roast chicken for friends. It was one of the first times I had attempted to cook a roast chicken dinner without my mum being present. I never paid much attention to my mother when she made gravy and therefore didn't have the confidence to make it myself. I placed all the food (the roast chicken, roast vegetables and a salad) out on the table. I was very proud of myself. One of the guests enquired in a not-so-quiet voice, 'Where's the gravy? You cannot have a roast without gravy!' I felt a pang. It was true, I had always had gravy growing up. Yet one of the other guests replied that they never had gravy with roasts. We then had a big discussion about how some people grew up having gravy with roasts and so that is what they expected when they had a roast, while others didn't, and therefore they didn't expect to get gravy. I found it interesting that the food we grow up with shapes our expectations of how food should be served.

I grew up with cereal, porridge or toast for breakfast. Some days, mostly on the weekend, we got a cooked breakfast. When I developed a friendship with a Swedish girl, I was introduced to another sort of dining experience. They had cheese on a type of cracker for breakfast! It amazed me how and why they chose to eat something like that for breakfast. I thought it rather odd and chose to continue to eat cereal instead. Having grown up a bit more now, I am more open to trying new things. I now look forward to trying different breakfasts when travelling to different countries.

You are laying down the foundations of what your children will choose to eat. When you say, 'Let's have a snack' and serve the typical Western snack food of crackers, chips, biscuits, etc, that will be the food they snack on. That will be the food they will gravitate towards when they become adults. A snack will be synonymous with processed food.

What if you changed the food you serve your children? What if you served mainly fresh fruit or vegetable sticks at snack times? Your children would then grow up with the belief that a snack is a piece of fruit or some nuts. I am not saying they will only choose these snacks, but they are more likely to choose fresh food over processed food when you instil a habit of having mainly fresh food for snacks.

Being a conscious parent implies that we are making decisions for our children, yet 95 per cent of our lives are operated unconsciously. To truly become a conscious parent when it comes to food and nutrition we need to examine our beliefs about food. This includes what and why we eat certain foods. Why do we in Western cultures typically have cereal and toast for breakfast? Why do we have our biggest meal at the end of the day? Why do we eat crackers and chips for snacks? Why do we have gravy with a roast? I am not saying by asking ourselves these questions we have to change the way we do things, but just being aware of why you choose to have cereal every morning will help you to teach your children about developing a healthy relationship with food.

OUR REJECTION IS THEIR REJECTION

Mirror neurons, as described earlier, have to answer for a lot. Adults unknowingly influence what children like or dislike in food. Studies show that children model their food preferences and eating behaviours on their parents.[5] What food do you not like so, therefore, not give to your children? Or do you give your children these foods but screw up your face when you give it to them? Children see your rejection and it becomes their rejection. They literally create neural pathways in their brains that tell them they do not like that food, all because they observe the way you react.

Ben doesn't like tomatoes. I am not fussed either way, but I have not exposed my children to them. Instead of being open to my children liking tomatoes, I once caught myself deciding that they didn't like them. I said to a friend, who offered my children some small cherry tomatoes as a snack, 'Oh, no thank you. They don't like them.' They had never tried them before, yet I made a decision that they would not like them based on what I expected them to like and not to like! I was directly influencing their preferences based on my own preferences. I have also done this with food that I have given them yet looked at them, waiting for their reaction with a nervous look on my face . . . No wonder they didn't like it. It may not have been because they actually had a huge aversion to the taste, but because I was showing them that it wasn't a food they should like.

Children also tend to have to *develop* a taste for food: the more you give it to them the more they will like it (see chapter seven). If you do not offer your children certain food they will not develop a taste for it, and therefore when they get to an age when they can start making conscious choices for themselves, they may try it once and say 'Oh no, that is not good.' You have probably done this when experiencing foods in different cultures. In New Zealand we grow up on Marmite or Vegemite. Only a few rare individuals do not like them (that may be their parents' influence as well!), yet give Marmite toast to an American and they will be disgusted by it! Just as I was when I tasted the much-loved Japanese natto for the first time. My mouth still salivates thinking of the taste.

BE OPEN

It can be shocking the first time you hear yourself say something to your children that your parents said to you when you were growing up. It is acceptable to complain about your parents, so to realise that you are like them is confronting.

When I was younger I absorbed how my parents interacted. In my family, my parents have old-school gender roles. When people came to our house for dinner or lunch, Mum cooked and Dad entertained. This worked and continues to work very well for them and they are both happy doing 'their own thing'. My mum loves to cook and if Dad came in to help, he would just upset her rhythm — she likes to be in control in the kitchen. This is what I grew up with. This is what I knew. This is how I am. Except for one thing — I also love to sit down and entertain, and I have felt, in the past, rather resentful that I did all the cooking and Ben, although offering to help, did all the entertaining. For years I thought this was my role, to cook and clean up, while Ben's role was to entertain. I became a bit of a martyr about it until I recognised I was filling a role that I had learnt from my parents, which I never questioned. I had a belief that I should cook and clean, even though I didn't fully enjoy it.

Once I realised and understood this, I began to form a balance.

Now when we have guests for dinner, I accept help in preparing dinner when Ben asks, and I leave the clean-up for both of us to do once our guests have left. This way I get to enjoy the night more. Nobody had ever told me that I was expected to cook and clean, but I had absorbed these lessons from my parents. It was not until I was able to critically think about my beliefs that I saw a different way of doing things — a way that suited me better.

The point is, you can only change what you are aware of. I could have gone my whole life thinking that my role was to cook and clean and not take a break to properly entertain. I could have wondered why my mother, aunties and sisters did it so happily, and concluded something was wrong with me because I wasn't happy doing it. Becoming aware of the gender roles I had learnt through osmosis when I was young freed me to see how I could do things better for myself.

Your beliefs about food shape how you parent. By becoming aware of how you see food you are free to do things better for yourself and for your children. You can choose to do things to suit you and your family, rather than just falling into ways of doing things because that is how you grew up.

Whether you like to admit it or not, your parents, caregivers and other significant adults in your life have had a large influence on what you think about food, from what they said about food, the experiences around food they created, to what they said to you and even what you overheard them saying. Until the age of eight, you absorbed these messages without critically thinking if they were true or false.

I don't offer my children Coke or any fizzy drink and we don't have juice in the house. I drink water with my meals and so does Ben. It is just a habit, and Coke or juice are not part of our lives. And because it is not on our radar it is not on our children's radar, either. These neural connections of drinking something fizzy and sweet like Coke, having it as a treat, or any awareness of it, have not been built in our children's brains.

I was at a family gathering recently where my six-year-old daughter walked in and asked for water. My husband's cousin replied, 'Oh, that is so good she doesn't ask for Coke.' My reply was, 'She doesn't even know what Coke is.' I don't think she quite comprehended that someone would not drink Coke, not only not in front of her children, but ever.

On the flip side, Ben and I enjoy a beer now and again. Our children see it and they quite often ask for one themselves. It is easy to be dismissive about trying beer, because it has alcohol in it. Yet I am fully aware that, although our children may not grow up drinking Coke or beer, as an adult they are more likely to have the occasional beer than they are likely to drink Coke, simply because they have grown up seeing us drink beer and not Coke.

What we do as parents and adults will influence our children's future habits. If you want your children not to drink Coke, don't drink it yourself.

This goes beyond drinking Coke. Going back to Amanda and her daughter Susie, Susie was learning everything off Amanda, yet Amanda could not see how her anxiety or her food choices affected her daughter. Let's face it, children will do what you do and not as you say! If you see any habits or ways your child interacts with food, be it sneaking food, snacking all the time or not eating properly at mealtimes, wolfing down food and not chewing it, whatever it is, look to yourself first. Have they learnt this habit from you?

Although I kept the house pretty clean of sweet food, I would eat it or sneak it when my children were not around. I think that if I am going to eat a food, it is free game for my children, so I tried not to eat sweet food around them. Problem solved, right? But children see things that we don't think they see. Huxley used to pick up on my habit and she would go sweet crazy when she was around anything sweet. When I admitted to myself that maybe she was learning off me, her relationship with sweet food slowly changed.

Becoming aware of our own beliefs around food is the foundation to encouraging our children to have a healthy relationship with food.

It is the starting point. Knowing that a lot of our beliefs about food are not based on truths but from our experiences when we were young ourselves puts us at an advantage to choose differently for our children, when they are themselves forming beliefs about food that they will have as adults and that they will teach their children. It is an ongoing cycle and you are in a position to change not only your beliefs around food but society's beliefs as a whole.

You can gain all the knowledge you want but experiencing that knowledge is the way forward. Start with the following action steps, then if you want to take it a step further keep an eye and ear out for how we as a society teach our kids about food. You will encounter many messages that we as a whole are teaching children about food without even realising it. You will realise it though, and this will be the start of a different journey for you and your children.

Open your mind to the way you have been limiting what you expect your children to eat and enjoy eating. From this new viewpoint you can move forward. Change what you expect from your children and maybe they will end up eating *and* enjoying more food.

Encouraging your children to have a healthy relationship with food starts with you. Your beliefs about food, your body, and when and how you should eat will directly and indirectly affect your children's beliefs. Stephen Covey, author of *The Seven Habits of Highly Effective People,* defines responsibility as the ability to respond. To be able to respond to our children's needs without the use of food starts with awareness. When you shed light on your past, your beliefs about food will enable you to take responsibility for how you influence your children's eating habits. Although you may not feel this way yet, I think it is exciting. Now you will be aware of your beliefs and have the choice to instil the habits you want in your children.

ACTION STEPS

We limit what our children eat because of how we, as adults, perceive food. What we think affects our children. We can also open up our children to new food experiences by changing our own beliefs around food. Reflect on your beliefs around food. Get out a journal and jot down the answers to these questions:

1. Do you treat yourself with unhealthy food?
2. What for you is 'treat' food? (Is it synonymous with 'unhealthy' food?)
3. What do you think is 'kid-friendly food'?
4. What food do you think children would never like?
5. Do you only serve vegetables and healthy food in a certain way (e.g. with sugar or tomato sauce) because you think that children are more likely to eat them?
6. What kind of food is synonymous with snacks, breakfast, lunch or dinner?
7. What food have you assumed your children won't like because you or your partner don't like it?
8. Do your children have any undesirable actions around food? If so, have they learnt them from you?

CHAPTER TWO

THE SPOTLIGHT'S ON YOU

Growing up, I played a lot of basketball. My first coach had a knack for teaching first-timers about the fundamentals of playing basketball; breaking down the layup was where he shined. But as I and my teammates got better at playing and understood the game better, although I didn't quite understand it at the time, our confidence in him as a coach decreased. Looking back I can see why. He had the fundamentals, but yet when he tried to demonstrate a more complicated move, he was a bit uncoordinated. He didn't have the ability to walk his talk and then when we questioned him, he would dismiss our questions and reinforce that it was *his* way.

However, my next coach, although she maybe didn't have the fundamentals of my first coach, had one thing he didn't have: flexibility. She could see that she was not going to get everything right but made it clear that she was learning, too. She instilled in me that to be good at anything you need to keep practising. This is the same with any skill, whether it is a basketball skill or a life skill.

As parents we don't need to get everything right to be able to teach our kids. Although teaching your kids to have a healthy relationship with food starts with you, it doesn't mean you need to have everything perfect before you can be great at teaching your children.

Let's be honest for a moment. We are never going to be a perfect parent. We are parenting our children for an unknown future based on what we have learnt in the past. Talk about impossible!

One of the fundamentals of parenting is teaching kids that they are not 'fixed' in a certain state. This gives them an inbuilt belief system where they know they can change if they choose to. For example, if we as parents have a tendency to lose control of our anger, we can either choose to try to hide this from our children — but let's be honest, kids see everything — or we can choose to explain to them how we are trying to express our anger in healthier ways, that we are trying to change. That was the difference between my basketball coaches. One tried to hide that he was a bit uncoordinated, losing my respect and that of my teammates. The other was open in saying she knew how and what to do, but had not mastered it herself — she was still practising. Our respect for her was immense.

In this chapter the spotlight is on you — not to highlight where you are going wrong, but simply to bring to your awareness what subtle messages your children are picking up from you around food.

I am sure you know, or are a part of, a family who has similar mannerisms. I was rewatching a video blog I had put out, and although I never thought I looked like my sister, I couldn't help but see her in my actions. It wasn't anything I was saying, but what I was doing, that looked similar. I am also sure you have had moments when you stop mid-sentence because you can see that you are waving your hands exactly like your mother or father used to. Children look up to their parental figures and learn through everything they do and how they behave. The mirror neurons we discussed earlier have a lot to do with this. Food is no exception.

If you eat a variety of food, chances are your children will. If you like to try new food, chances are your children will, too. If you snack lots and sneak food, or even if you have some emotional attachment to food, chances are your children will, too. Even the way you see food or mealtimes has a profound influence on your children's taste preferences and habits around food.

This chapter is about becoming aware of what you do around food and how you interact with food, so you can be like the basketball coach who was aware of her limitations yet showed me how I needed to practise — even as an adult — in order to grow. What a powerful life lesson for your kids.

ARE YOU ADVENTUROUS?

Variety

If you eat only a narrow range of food on a regular basis, expect your children to be the same. When we eat a variety of foods, our children are more likely to eat more variety. They will see that eating a variety of foods is normal. If they see you eating a food, it automatically becomes not a 'new food' and is more likely to be accepted into their diet. If they see you trying new foods, any food, they themselves are more likely to try new food.

I used to serve my children healthy food, yet the day I saw that four-year-old eat a tomato, I was faced with a question — do I give my children a variety of food? Or, more importantly, do I eat a variety? I didn't. I served the kids mostly carrots, cucumber and capsicums, and a lot of the time I just cut them into sticks. I did this because I knew they would eat them, and I really wanted them to eat some vegetables. I didn't want to have a confrontation with them over not wanting to eat other vegetables. Although I ate more of a variety of vegetables, I labelled some of it as not 'kid food', so I hesitated giving it to my children. When I started to give them more variety through different vegetables, either cooked differently or in new meals, I saw an increase in their eating of the vegetables I had once labelled as not 'kid-friendly'.

I also noticed that although I did eat more of a variety of foods than the kids, I also had gotten into the habit of eating the same food or type of food day in and day out. First of all, it's easier to cook what you know, either in terms of the style of cooking or the ingredients used. I knew how to cook with certain foods but others, like eggplant, were not on my radar. When I was at the supermarket with three children, my mission was to get in and get out without tears or tantrums — choosing a different vegetable that most probably would just lay in the fridge until it got rotten was not at the top of my priority list! However, simply being aware that I was subtly teaching my children through what I was doing, means I now pick different food items from time to time. This is not a daily or even a weekly occurrence for me; I would find it too overwhelming if I was trying to cook with something I was not familiar with all the time. I take it slow and when I see something which might be a lesson that would benefit the kids at certain stages I make sure I add it to my diet first.

For example, on one occasion I got a few pictures of vegetables that we didn't eat on a regular basis and I asked what one they would like to 'experiment' with. They chose eggplant, so we went about experimenting with eggplant and the different ways to cook and prepare it. They didn't like any of them, but that was not the lesson!

Also, I started to learn more about other styles of cooking. Once I wanted to learn to cook a good curry. I got lots of recipes and trialled different ones. Two of our three kids now like curry and the other one is not that fussed. Again, that is not the lesson — the lesson is bringing variety not only into their diets but into ours as well.

New food

When a client, April, asked me how to get her child to try new food, I asked if she tried new food herself. She said yes, but when I then asked her about the last time she tried a new dish at a restaurant or cooked something new, she was stumped.

While adults tend to eat more variety, they often still stick to what they know. This is the same for children. If you don't try eating or cooking new and different food, they do not have a role model. They are not too sure how to react to new food or even why they should try it.

It seems that children from about three years old become unsure of new food. Even if they accepted a variety of food before the age of three, children can go through a stage from the ages of three to five where they are more suspicious of new food.[6] Some may see this as an excuse not to give their children new food. I see it as being the *best* time to introduce new food. My reasoning is that trying new things is like using a muscle — if we exercise it we get stronger.

Ben and I love to have people over for dinner. At one time we had gone a few months without having people over, so Ben decided to fill up five out of seven nights with entertaining different guests. After the first dinner I was tired. I wasn't looking forward to the next few days, having to keep the house clean, cook different meals and make small talk. When I mentioned this to Ben, he said, 'Yeah, I know. But the more we do it the better and easier it will become.' Sure enough, by the end of the week, I was not half as tired as I had been on the first day, but my enjoyment levels increased over the week. By the end I was so much more relaxed and less stressed compared to the start of the week. I had exercised the entertaining muscle and it had gotten stronger.

It is the same with introducing new food to children. When we first try it, it can go poorly, but the more you do it, the more you will find what works for your children. In the upcoming chapters, I also cover what language to use to help them find it enjoyable (and decrease your stress levels) during these interactions.

Introducing new food in the years between three and five has the added bonus of normalising trying new food. Your children will not even have to question if they want to try new food or not — they will always welcome new food with at least one bite without encouragement from you!

Trying

When Ben and I and the kids were travelling around America, one of our stops was San Francisco. This amazing city has a great Chinatown. Having walked for a few hours we were famished and decided to go to one of the many restaurants there. Ben likes to be adventurous when he orders at a restaurant and either orders the most unusual dish on the menu or the waitress's favourite. That day he decided to get the most unusual dish: chicken feet. I kid you not. There were some locals sitting behind us of Chinese descent and even they were having a laugh at one of their friends getting chicken feet!

I had one of two options: be the mother in the corner turning up her nose at the dish, or get over myself and my past beliefs and see it as an awesome opportunity to teach the kids about trying new food.

This situation was quite hard, as I physically wanted to gag as the chicken feet were placed on the table. Looking at it objectively, this was a reaction that I had learnt and I didn't want to teach my children the same reaction. Ben also got a bit of a shock when they were placed on the table — they didn't look that appealing. However, without being dishonest, when Huxley asked if I thought the dish looked nice, I replied, 'No, I don't like the look of it, but I have found that sometimes when food doesn't look that great, once I try it, it tastes great.'

Ben tried the chicken feet first, I was next and then all the children tried it. I found it interesting that our youngest was the one who didn't turn her nose up at all, just tucked on in. Rasmus and I decided that one bite was enough, while Ben and Huxley finished a few feet between them.

I am not too sure if we would order chicken feet again, but that is not the point. This was a big lesson in trying new food. They saw that I, in particular, was not keen on the look of the food, yet I tried it anyway — it wasn't about liking it or pretending to like it, it was about trying. A belief they started to carve into their subconscious on this day was that even if you don't like the look of foods you try them, all because they saw Ben and me do it.

YOUR EATING STYLE

Snacking

Over one-quarter of food eaten by children is in the form of snacks. Sweetened products such as cakes, biscuits, tarts, muffins, etc and sweetened beverages are the major contributors to snacks. I am frequently asked by parents how to stop their children from filling up between meals. I ask a couple of questions:

Firstly — do you graze? If children see you doing something or not doing something, they are more likely to do it or not do it themselves.

Mary was a parent who approached me after a talk one evening. She asked how she could get her children to eat more at the dinner table. She said that her children ate more at snack times. When I asked her about her own eating, her response was, 'Who gets time to sit down to eat? I am always eating standing.' Just saying it, she realised what message she was sending to her children. She made an effort to eat at the dinner table and her children followed suit. After all, children just want to be around their parents. That is why the designated 'playroom' never gets used — unless you are in there, too.

Secondly — do you let your children go hungry? Most parents will be confused by this question. 'Of course I don't!' answered one mum at a talk I was giving. We think that when our children say 'I'm hungry!' we have to drop everything we are doing and get them something to eat. God forbid they should go hungry! I always ask parents, 'What are you so afraid of?' Let's be honest — unless they have not eaten for an entire day they are not likely to be so hungry that they need food straight away. Letting them wait half an hour or an hour will not kill them.

I also think it is good for children to learn how to comprehend hunger and deal with it. It took me a long time to recognise that the sensation of hunger I felt was connected with my short wick now and again! Although it should not be a goal for your children to get so hungry they have a tantrum, just know if this does occur it can be a great opportunity to teach them about their hunger levels and coping mechanisms for such occasions in the future. Start by talking about your hunger levels. Show them it is normal to be hungry but also it is normal to stop eating when you don't feel hungry anymore. The more you can explain and bring in your experiences to your children the more they will start to make connections for themselves.

Thirdly — what snacks do you eat and give your children? I always used to have crackers handy. I considered them prime snack food. They were easy and I knew the children liked them and I liked them as well. When I started to really look at what I was feeding my children, I knew that crackers were not that great for them nutritionally. I thought the ease (oh, the ease!) outweighed the nutritional value (and I secretly talked myself into believing that crackers have great fibre content). However, when I also started to think about what habits I was teaching them I had a radical shift in the type of snacks I gave my children.

When we give children snacks that are white, processed and full of who-knows-what, we are teaching them the habit of filling up on processed food between meals. This becomes their habit. On the flip side, when giving your children 'real' food as snacks (vegetable sticks, fruit, nuts, boiled eggs, etc), they will form the habit of eating real food as snacks.

But to reinforce what this chapter is about, it starts with you. If you are filling up on snacks that are not real foods, your children will see this and that will become their normal. If snacks are an issue with your kids, then start with what you snack on first — be that role model.

Sneaking food

Do your kids sneak food? A client came to see me with the primary concern that her children were sneaking food. She had tried to develop an open and honest relationship with her kids, as she had sneaked food when she was younger and didn't want that for her children. Yet they did.

Children sneak food for a variety of reasons. The first, which we will cover in chapter three, is about restriction and control: when we are told we cannot have something, most of the time we want it even more. But another reason, which parents don't often think about, is that they sneak food themselves. Like I did.

I grew up sneaking food. It was just what my sisters and I did. Whether it was Granddad's chocolate or jelly crystals out of the pantry, I remember many times sneaking food that 'wasn't allowed'. Yet I still did it as a grown-up. I didn't want the kids to have certain foods, so when they were not around I would sneak a packet or two of chocolate biscuits into the supermarket trolley and eat them when they were not looking. I was sneaking food from them! Although I find this hard to admit to you, I know that a lot of parents do it and it is not even questioned. Of course we sneak food, especially when it is food we don't want our children to have!

Looking at it plainly, I am sure you can see how sneaking food from your children is setting them up for the same behaviour. Although I never let on, I saw the chocolate biscuits go into our trolley as a young child, yet whenever I went to find them in the pantry . . . they were never there. I am not sure if my parents were deliberately trying to sneak food they didn't want us to eat, but I interpreted it like that. Sneaking food for myself as a child, although I knew it was 'naughty', was still something that I considered normal.

Slow eating

I can still remember my heart racing as I gulped down the food. Was I beating her? Chew faster, I thought. She only has one potato left and, gosh, I have two — can I do it? Ah, just missed out. But I was close, maybe next time.

My mother ate fast. My mum is a great cook and likes to make sure everyone has what they want and need. She is the mum who prepares three different meats, five different salads and will have some sort of back-up just in case the food — made to feed 25 people when only 10 are present — disappears. She worries so much about other people that she will rarely sit down for an entire meal. I guess that is why she eats fast. She is the last to start and the first one to finish and this means she can get everyone else sorted.

I must have been about 10 when I first remember racing her to finish. I thought it was an amazing skill to be a fast eater. As I said before, I was a kid who would run everywhere to cut downtime and eating was no different. How boring it was to sit down and eat slowly!

As I grew older I became aware that eating slowly and chewing food thoroughly helps digestion, which flows on to a whole list of beneficial health outcomes. I tried to slow down. It was hard! I didn't fully grasp how much I needed to slow down until my son ate a steak in two bites. He raced through his food without chewing it. Being the neurotic mother and nutritionist I am, I started to think of how bad it was for his stomach, his intestines and him in general. I was quite aware that I ate fast, so I didn't have to question where he was getting it from! I had adopted the same habits as my mother. I would fuss about, be the last one sitting, the first one finishing and I could not tell you when I last sat through an entire meal from start to finish. I decided I needed to change, if not for me, then at least for Rasmus.

I found success by not calling everyone to the table unless the food was ready — everyone's food, not just the children's meal. I also set the table so there was water, sauces and everything we needed at the start, eliminating the need to get up during meals. I then aimed to be the slowest eater. I did this by putting my knife and fork down between bites, and if we had a chopstick-friendly meal, then we used them. Although Rasmus still eats his food rapidly, he is getting better. By slowing down at mealtimes I have inadvertently given them a better experience. I am more present to respond to the children, because I now have an expectation that I am in my seat eating for as long as it takes for the children to eat. This has meant a huge improvement in our mealtime experience as a family — just because I made an effort to slow down my eating.

YOUR RELATIONSHIP WITH FOOD

Emotional eating

Do you eat for any reason other than hunger? If you do, you are teaching your children to do the same. You may not recognise that you use food in an emotional way because you may not be the 'typical' comfort-eater.

Over the next week, before you eat, stop and ask yourself: Am I hungry or am I eating for another reason? You may be surprised with what you find. Quite often we have one or two emotions connected to eating. You may equally be surprised that your children are developing the same habits.

Remembering back to mirror neurons and children's brains being open to all impressions at a young age will help you to put this into context. When we are bored and keep going to the cupboards to see what we can snack on, kids see this as a normal reaction to boredom! If whenever we are going through a hard time we go to the supermarket and get a tub of ice-cream to polish off, children will interpret this as a normal reaction to feeling down or coping with hard times. A tub of ice-cream or other food can become an emotional filler.

This is a thorny issue for many adults, because most people have some sort of emotional eating patterns. When people become aware of their pattern they can get overwhelmed as they don't want their children to experience the same sort of emotional eating, but stopping this cycle is in the 'too-hard basket'. Some will then start resorting to sneaking food — although we have seen that this is not a great habit either.

So what can be done? Remember back to my basketball coaches. You don't need to get everything right; just by being aware of the issue and making it known that you are trying to change, or even by acknowledging that it is not a good habit to have, you are giving your children the most empowering lesson there is.

I ate sugar for the excitement. At the times I was most bored in my life, sugar was a crutch. When I didn't have time to do things I felt excited about, such as mountain biking, I would turn to sugar to offer me some excitement, to deter the boredom I was feeling. To help keep this bad habit in check and to avoid teaching my children the habit of eating sweets out of boredom, I tried keeping a sugar-free house. I was pretty strict on it. No child of mine was going to like sugar! However, I was forced to admit that I was not getting something quite right when my eldest daughter would get candy-crazy at children's parties or at other people's houses. She would sing at the top of her voice, 'IIIII love caaaaaaandy!' I found it quite confronting and would often get disproportionately annoyed at her. I also found it confusing, as she often wouldn't actually eat the sweets or cake, often saying, 'Oh, this is too sweet for me.' The *thought* of candy was more appealing for her than the actual taste.

At that time, I could not see how my own emotional-eating pattern was affecting her. Fast-forward a few years, and my emotional sugar-eating pattern is no more. (A lot of people have asked how I have altered my sugar-eating ways. Going through the five-step habit changer I outline in chapter twelve, one sugary item at a time, was a long process but very effective!) And my daughter doesn't get so sweet-crazy.

Previously, although I kept no sugar in the house, she would have seen me devour a dessert when out for dinner, or go back for thirds or possibly fourths when eating dessert at my mother's house. Now she sees me trying the dessert but not eating the whole thing, or at least not eating it like it was my first meal after being stranded on a desert island. She now sees me talking about how when I am craving some sugar, on a deeper level I recognise it is because I need more excitement. After choosing to go for a mountain-bike instead I then explain how that has satisfied my appetite and I don't have the craving anymore.

More than that, she has picked up on my energy around sugary food. It is just another food item — not more, and most of the time less, appealing than a carrot. Freeing myself of my emotional attachment to sugar has shaped her food choices.

Your fears are often manifested in your children. If you are worried about an emotional attachment to food that your children have, ask yourself: Do I have this same emotional attachment?

The spotlight is on you. What you do in a normal day, the variety in your diet, whether or not you welcome trying new foods with open arms, whether you snack or graze often, or if emotional eating fuels your day, will be creating a blueprint for how your children interact with food. Your relationship with food will impact on their ability to develop a healthy relationship with food.

YOUR RELATIONSHIP WITH YOUR BODY

Eating affects us all. Eating directly affects body weight. How you perceive your body image and your identity surrounding your size can negatively (and positively) affect your relationship with food. This then flows on to your children.

Parents who have issues around body image can negatively influence their children to develop the same issues. If you have anxiety around food or your body, this energy can affect your children's relationship with food.[7]

On a particular sunny day I took the three kids for a walk at the beach. There was a short, steep climb to a lookout that had views of a long, sandy beach. It was about a 15-minute calf-burning uphill climb and a five-minute bounce down. Steps were carved in some sections to make it easier to climb. As we were walking down I heard Huxley, my eldest, exclaim 'Look Mum, I'm an adult!' She was walking down the stairs, taking one step at a time.

It was not the first time I had heard her or other children say this. Thinking back to my own childhood I remember the excitement of 'getting older' very well. Adults seemed to have everything they wanted: they went to sleep when they wanted, they could drive a car, they could do what they wanted, they could eat what they wanted.

Children want to be adults. You are the adult in their life that they look up to. They don't know what it is like to be an adult so they get their cues from you. The beliefs you hold about your body, and therefore your relationship with food, influence your children. As we have seen in the previous pages, if you use food for emotional reasons, or if you sneak food, they will pick up on this and interpret this as being part and parcel with being an adult. But it goes deeper.

Like it or not, most women are dissatisfied with their body image.[8] Often this body fixation is connected with food, in the way you eat and what you eat. If you are in this boat, confronting your issues with your body and food will help you to recognise the same patterns that either have or could potentially develop in your children.

You cannot fix what you don't know is broken. In becoming aware of your limiting beliefs, you are open to growth. After reading this chapter you may start to see your own beliefs being reflected in your children and want to change yourself. If you do, that's great. But you don't even need to fix your issues — sometimes just becoming aware of them is enough.

Body image

How do you see yourself? What is your body image?

Obesity runs in families. It has a lot to do with the type of food that parents choose to eat and consequently give their children. But I am sure you all know of overweight adults who eat very healthily, and I am sure you know of lean children who eat only 'kid-friendly food'. What is the difference between the two?

Mentality. I am sure most of you have heard the saying 'you get what you think about'. If I think of myself as the 'big girl', I will be big. I will self-sabotage any well-intentioned healthy-eating efforts.

Even if you are lean or an ideal weight, what is your relationship with food? How do you keep your weight 'in check'? Do you eat whatever you like or do you have to 'control' what you eat? Do you count calories? Do you feel naughty eating a piece of chocolate cake? Do you or your friends say 'I won't have a slice of that, because I am being "good"'?

I was at a three-year-old's birthday party. Pizza and ice-cream cake were served. I took a piece of pizza and it was horrible. (I am a bit of a pizza snob. If it is not top quality I won't eat it. This wasn't top quality.) However, I did the polite thing, what I was raised to do, and ate it . . . all! Then came the ice-cream cake. The pizza had already made me feel not so flash, so I declined. I am one of those weird people who is not a big fan of ice-cream. Even as a kid I could take it or leave it. So then the comments started, 'Oh, you're so good. I don't have that sort of willpower, no wonder you're so thin.' Then the looks, like I was 'that person' who had so much self-control. Apparently, someone like that doesn't have any fun!

I joke about it, but we all do it. We negatively judge someone who does something that we perceive as 'good', to make ourselves feel better. When I was at university, I had a friend, Kim, who was a healthy weight. She was like most of us: she didn't have legs that went 'all the way up' and her tummy wasn't completely flat. But she was, well, normal. One night Kim and I walked into a party and this model-like girl appeared. She had classic runway potential. She was thin and everything the magazines glorify. My friend whispered in a not-so-quiet voice, 'Oh gosh, eat a doughnut!' Even though I was a bit mortified with her comment, my thought was similar: 'Well, she has a great body, she must have issues.'

I know this is ringing true for a lot of you. Somewhere along the way we have bought into the idea that if we are not six foot tall with legs like Elle Macpherson, we are not good enough. We compare ourselves with others and when we do see someone who seems to have a 'great' body, we conclude that they must have 'issues'. We pick others apart in an attempt to make ourselves feel better about what we have.

I could sit here all day and argue where this is stemming from (the media, etc), but when it comes down to it, most of us have the same 'issues' as our mothers or fathers, whoever it is we identify with most. When we become completely satisfied and confident in our bodies, we judge others less. Whether we are vocal or internal with these judgements, our children will pick up on them. When we become confident in our own bodies we have more of a chance to raise girls and boys who are confident in their bodies. This in turn positively affects their relationship with food.

ACTION STEPS

In their book *Intuitive Eating: A Revolutionary Program That Works*, Evelyn Tribole and Elyse Resch point to eight core emotions that can trigger or influence food consumption: nurture, distraction, comfort, resolve, anxiety, loneliness, boredom and anger. As discussed above, sugar was my cure for boredom.

Your children's food habits can be affected by the way you interact with food. Think about how you use food and if your children are being affected by it. Over the next few days think about how and when you have food. Get out the journal you started in chapter one and jot down the answers to these questions:

1. Do you eat a variety of food?
2. Do you try new foods in front of your children?
3. Do you have any body issues? If so, how does this influence what you eat?
4. Are you eating for any other reasons than hunger?
5. Which emotions (nurture, distraction, comfort, resolve, anxiety, loneliness, boredom or anger) influence your eating?
6. If you have identified emotions in question four, what are your earliest memories of eating in that way — write with as much detail as possible.

By answering these questions you will start to shed light on your relationship with food and how this may flow onto your children. You can use these answers as a way to pinpoint the areas in your diet where you may like to develop a healthier relationship with food within yourself.

CHAPTER THREE

PARENTING STYLES

There are many ways to parent. We choose the way we parent based on our past experiences, our future expectations and our current situation. I am not going to sit here and pretend I know what is best for you, your children and your situation. But I will give you something to ponder. I will introduce you to differing parenting styles and what researchers have concluded with regard to how parenting creates positive eating patterns.

Your parenting style — what you say, what you do and how you interact with your children — will influence their love or hate of healthy food. I know you want the best for your children; you would not be reading this book otherwise. Yet sometimes the way you encourage children to eat healthy food can affect their eating patterns detrimentally. Again, this is not about blame, it is about becoming aware: aware of where you sit as a parent and if you are choosing, or are falling into, this way of parenting.

FOUR STYLES

There is a whole body of research dedicated to how parents raise their children and the effectiveness of differing parenting styles. Researchers such as Diana Baumrind, expanded on by Eleanor Maccoby and John Martin, have identified four parenting styles: neglectful, permissive, authoritarian and authoritative.[9]

Neglectful parents are uninvolved and don't tend to impose any boundaries on their children. Eating times have no structure and children are left to eat what they want and when they want. Parents can be neglectful for a few reasons, the most obvious being they are so involved in their own lives that they forget about their kids. Chances are, if you are reading this book, this is not you! However, just because you are not a neglectful parent all the time doesn't mean you have not had some moments or days when you let your kids do what they wanted, when they wanted. If you think this is you, it is important to identify the situations when you become neglectful and to have coping strategies to put in place so you don't become neglectful when these situations arise.

Permissive parents are nurturing and involved, yet they are reluctant to impose rules and standards on their children. These parents prefer to let children regulate themselves, and although they provide children with structure and mealtimes, they will serve whatever the children want to eat. If children do not like what is on their plate, the permissive parent will keep preparing food until the children get what they want.

We often get permissive when it comes to mealtimes when we are afraid that our children have not eaten enough — or anything. We prepare a meal and they don't like the look of it. Because we want them to eat something, anything to help them grow or even just sleep through the night, we may then either make them something else, like another meal or even toast, so we are satisfied they have had something to eat.

In my experience, when parents fall into being permissive around food it is because they feel an overwhelming desire to nurture and provide for their children and their awareness is centred on their children eating enough in that moment.

Authoritarian parents demand a lot from their children and provide them with strict and controlling rules and regulations. These parents set boundaries for their children and are very rigid and unresponsive to the child's individual needs. Researchers have found that parents being less sensitive and more controlling interferes with children's autonomy and can result in children being more likely to eat in the absence of hunger.[10] This habit is one of the core issues that affect people's relationship with food.

In my experience, an authoritarian style around food can manifest for a couple of reasons. Firstly, after a busy day looking after and attending to kids, work, home life, etc, parents will cook a meal that is known to be healthy for both their children's growing bodies and their growing minds. Yet, sitting down at the dinner table, exhausted, the kids turn up their noses even before they try it. This can lead to an overwhelming surge of emotions that causes parents to demand the kids eat: anything from one decent bite to finishing everything on their plate. Secondly, parents who adopt this style often see parenting from the viewpoint of control — because parents know what is best — rather than from a viewpoint of guiding children to make their own decisions.

Authoritative parents are more nurturing and responsive. They show respect for the child and offer emotional support when needed, yet provide boundaries and expectations for their children. They are responsive to and supportive of their children.

I will use the term 'coaching parent' for authoritative parent from here on, as authoritarian and authoritative can get very confusing when used interchangeably.

Coaching parenting has been linked with successful child outcomes, producing qualities such as self-reliance and being socially accepted and academically successful. Children who are raised by parents who use a coaching style tend to have higher fruit and vegetable consumption and overall healthier eating patterns as adults.

Really, when you think about it, it is a no-brainer. Don't think of pink elephants — I bet you are thinking of pink elephants now. When parents say 'don't do' something, without a good reason, all children want to do it — some more than others, but there is always a bit of excitement: 'Ohhh, I wonder what is going to happen if I do it?'

A few years ago I had walked up a steep hill with my daughter and her cousin. On the top of this hill there was a lookout and a pretty steep drop. Huxley and her cousin were goofing around and it made me nervous. I asked them to stop many times, but it seemed to fall on deaf ears, and I was getting even more anxious and annoyed that they were not listening to me. Eventually, I walked them over to the drop-off and said in an empathetic tone, 'Look, I know it is fun to be rolling around here, but I am afraid that you will lose control and drop off this cliff. I really don't want you to hurt yourselves.' They both looked at the drop-off and at where they had been playing, then Huxley's cousin said, 'Should we go up there and play?' pointing to a much more level and safe area. Yes! Both had heard me when I asked them to stop goofing around, but they couldn't quite comprehend why I was saying 'don't do that'. Once they understood, they were quite happy to choose another place to have fun.

If you are reading about these parenting styles for the first time, you are probably thinking, 'Yep, it is confirmed, I am a good parent, I fall into the coaching boat.' I know I did. What is important here is not to be judgemental of yourself. Parents want the best for their children, and they do it in the way that they know how to, whether that is being permissive, neglectful, authoritarian or coaching. While coaching may be your 'go-to' style, I am sure you have, at times, used the other styles. This is not a time to judge yourself, it is an opportunity for growth.

I can, although sheepishly, admit that I have been permissive at times and authoritarian at times around food. I have been permissive when I have had a long day and don't have the energy to 'encourage' my children to eat. Sometimes I have used permissive parenting as a way to fit into a friend's or family member's way of parenting and to look like a good mother in their eyes.

I have been authoritarian sometimes, not so much in what I have said but what I have done. Rigid and unresponsive. Giving off a tone of, 'I don't care if you don't like what I have served. I have slaved away and you will eat this without complaining.' Creating a warm and responsive eating atmosphere has been the last thing I have felt like doing and this is okay, no one can be a perfect parent all the time. However, just by being aware of what tone I am using with my children, I have been able to see how this related to their behaviour at dinner times. You will, too.

From here you may decide, like myself, to work on being primarily a coaching parent. It is an effort, but you will be rewarded with not only happier children at mealtimes, but children who are more likely to choose to eat the foods you want them to!

COACHING NUTRITION

Science knows a lot about nutrition: from what food has in it to how it affects our body. We have knowledge of which foods make us gain weight, how different enzymes and gut flora and micronutrients behave in our bodies — you name it, we know it.

With all this knowledge, you would think we would have it all sorted, with everyone living in peak physical condition, and nutritional-related diseases, such as obesity, diabetes and heart disease, few and far between. Yet this is not the case. We have the most information ever about what constitutes a healthy diet, yet we are the unhealthiest we have ever been.

Our pursuit of knowledge has clouded our understanding of how to create health. It is not nutritional knowledge that we lack. Understanding the body and how nutrition affects it has been an area of study for many years, hoping to reverse, delay or even avoid certain diseases. Researchers have uncovered amazing amounts of information, from cinnamon's effect on blood glucose to sugar's effect on our cholesterol levels. Yet we remain fat, diseased and unhappy.

All parents want the best for their children. I am no different. I developed cancer in my early twenties. I also teach others how to eat. I was adamant that my children would love healthy foods and not entertain the unhealthy ones. I didn't want them to get sick like I had. Although I will never know what actually caused my cancer, I knew that nutrition was one area that could have played a large part. Nutrition was also one area that I thought I could control in my children.

My plan was simple: to feed my children healthy food on a daily basis. When they were offered food from others that was not in the 'plan', I would teach them that was 'bad' food. Even if they had a rebellious phase, I hoped they would come back to healthy food as adults. Not a bad plan. But thinking about it more, wanting more for my children, I saw that this plan was exactly what I had grown up with. I turned out fine, but I also had bulimia for seven years. I sneaked food, I devoured sweets and I felt enormous amounts of guilt and shame around food. I wanted more for my children.

My interest in helping parents to create a healthy relationship with food in their children comes from helping adults. I have seen, through many years of working one-on-one with people and giving seminars about nutrition, that *talking* nutrition is one thing but *coaching* nutrition is another ball game. Most people know what they *should* eat, yet when faced with a day-to-day decision they eat what they know they shouldn't. I am fascinated with this area and as I continued to read research on how to change habits, I realised that as a parent, instead of just *hoping* my children would like vegetables and healthy food when they grew up, I could shape their food preferences. Through working with adults I became aware of the beliefs I wanted to instil in my children.

I got out of my comfort zone and tried different methods of encouragement, ones that were new territory for me, to help my children eat a variety of healthy food. When I saw the impact I was making, I was hooked. *Coaching* my children to have a healthy relationship with food became a priority. I took more responsibility for their eating, and by taking responsibility for creating their eating habits (the *how*), instead of thinking about *what* they were eating, my responsiveness and attitude changed. I put in place different strategies that I could go to when I didn't have the energy to put into mealtimes, or when I just wanted them to eat the food I gave them without argument. I found that changing the way I gave food to my children has had a domino effect — tipping one item made all the others fall.

In the following pages we will examine how you may have used food in the past to enforce healthy eating and the possible consequences.

FOOD IS NOT JUST FOR NOURISHMENT

In *Mindless Eating,* researcher Brian Wansink identifies four ways parents, or 'nutritional gatekeepers' as he calls them, encourage their children to eat healthy food.

- The reward: 'If you finish this broccoli then you can have ice-cream.'
- The punishment: 'Finish all your veges or you can't use the iPad.'
- The guilt: 'Eat everything on your plate — think about all those children in Africa who have no food.'
- The comfort: 'Here, have this cupcake, it will make you feel better.'

I was walking around the supermarket with three children in tow: one in the trolley, one helping me push the trolley and one running up and down the aisles. I was already a little bit stressed as I thought I was going to be late for Huxley's soccer. I had a plan to get in and get out quickly. The reality of being in the supermarket with three children with half (or most) of my attention on them — distracting the little one so that she would continue to sit in the trolley, keeping an eye on the one that was running around, and having the trolley always pushed away from me by the third — meant I kept missing what I had gone in for. The amount of times I went back and forth up the same aisles was getting me worked up. I needed the children to be good, and using food as a bribe was an easy way to control their behaviour: 'Hey, if you kids are good, I will get you some dried mango.' Although I had not bribed the kids with lollies or other typical food that are used as treats, I knew they liked dried mango, so I used that. This was not the first time I had used it as a reward for 'being good'. It was easy and it worked. However, there came a day that I finally admitted to myself that, like it or not, I was using food to control my children. This action was creating a habit that was not in line with instilling a healthy relationship with food.

Do you use food for anything else but feeding your children? Are you like me and offer food as a treat or a reward to get your children to behave? 'Be good and I'll give you X'. Let's look at these four ways we, as parents or nutritional gatekeepers, use food, and what messages children can receive from them.

The reward

Food is often used as a reward to bribe children to be good. From sitting in the supermarket trolley to eating everything on their plate, the situations are endless.

Using food as a reward sets children up for a number of things. First of all, the reward is often sugar-laden or fried food. You are unconsciously telling your children that this food is good! Unhealthy food is put on a pedestal. This creates an expectation that this food tastes good. Even if they were not going to like it, they will definitely like it after you set it up as a reward. It can also set your children up for a lifetime of using food as a reward. Often they will be oblivious they are doing this.

This was highlighted to me when I was talking with a client who had struggled with her weight her whole life. She knew more or less what to eat and how it was her food choices that kept her overweight, but she couldn't help putting that food to her lips. You could argue that her willpower wasn't that good. But she had the most willpower I had seen in anyone — just not around food.

One of her turning points came when she realised that she used food as a reward. She had had a long day, doing three different jobs over 12 hours. As she was driving home and thinking how she had done a great job during the day, not only lasting the whole day but doing all her jobs in a great mood, she couldn't help but think, 'Good, I can get McDonald's.' She spoke of how, in that moment, she saw how she used food as a reward. She knew that McDonald's was an unhealthy option for her, yet that was her choice of reward — she had grown up with 'eat your greens and then you will get dessert'; 'collect 10 stickers for going potty and you will get McDonald's'. She didn't really feel like McDonald's, but this was her reward for her long day. Food was a reward that she had unconsciously bought into. From this moment on, McDonald's was on her mind.

Whether you are using food to reward your children after they have collected 10 stickers for doing chores around the house or you use it on the spur of the moment, like to get through the supermarket shopping — stop! This is a habit that will set your children up for anything but a healthy relationship with food. Instead of using food, use experiences — going to the park, going swimming, whatever your children like — just not food.

The punishment

Punishment is much like the reward, except it is used negatively: 'Finish your vegetables, otherwise there is no TV.' Unhealthy food is often used to reward your children and healthy food to punish them. The unhealthy food is put on a pedestal and the healthy food is made to instil a hate for it. My sister was made to finish her peas, even though she gagged on them. She had to finish her peas or else. To this day she will not even try peas, because it was used against her.

Using food as a punishment creates a negative association with this food. Have you ever said, 'Finish your ice-cream or you won't be getting any time on the iPad'? I am guessing not. By using food for punishment your children grow up with a negative association towards this food and tend not to choose this food later on in life. Even using the phrase 'finish your vegetables or else' can instil an underlying dislike for vegetables in general. Your children's expectations will be tainted even before they try them. Associating food with punishment is not part of instilling a healthy relationship with food.

The guilt

Guilt is another tool parents and caregivers use to encourage children to eat. The most common way I have seen it used is in statements like 'Think about all those people starving in Africa.'

When I think about that statement, I am baffled. It is a complete and utter guilt-trip. As an adult I can see that now. I am able to ask,

'What does me eating this food at this instance have to do with those in Africa? How will they benefit from me eating more?' But as a child I could not see it. I overheard an adult saying this to my children a few years ago, when the children were not old enough to comprehend it. Instinctively, I asked this person how my children eating more food would benefit the children in Africa. She was stumped. Luckily, she was very open and didn't take offence or try to justify her point of view. We got to discussing it and I can still remember the thought process spreading across her face. She had no idea why she said it; it was something her mother had told her and she thought it was a good way to encourage children to eat. She said it in an innocent way — but I question if the messages taken away by some children are innocent.

Huxley, who is old enough to comprehend guilt, turned to me sheepishly one day and asked about the starving people in Africa. We were travelling around a lot and were in and out of other people's homes, so we were eating what our hosts were eating. She had started eating toast with the crust taken off, as she had seen someone do this for her younger sister and wanted the same. On this day she was eating her crusts. I commented on it, and she turned to me very shyly (which is not her normal self) and said, 'Mum, all the children in Africa don't have any food.' As it turns out, one of her aunties had taken a dislike to her not eating her crusts, so used the guilt trip of 'starving African children' to get her to eat her crusts.

I was in full swing writing this book at the time, so was extra conscious of using guilt to get children to eat food. I was a little bit angry, but saw it as a chance to help Huxley. We talked about it, and I asked her how her not eating her crusts was going to save the children in Africa. She replied with a giggle, 'Not unless I send it to them.' From here the conversation turned to how we could actually help those people who had limited food, from raising money to inventing ways to purify water. It was a great conversation and one that I know impacted on her, as later on I heard her say to the aunty who had tried to guilt-trip her, 'Eating my crusts won't help them but my inventions may.'

In my past I have had a lot of guilt around food. I thought that when I was a guest in someone's house I should eat everything I was given, gagging down food when I not only didn't like it but felt it was repulsive. I did so because it would show how grateful I was. I would feel obliged to eat everything on my plate, because it showed I appreciated their cooking efforts. Even when I had control over my own servings and what I ate or didn't eat, for years I would finish everything on my plate. I would overeat so much that after dinner I would have to go and sit on the couch for half an hour because I was uncomfortably full. This wasn't a rare Christmas or birthday event — it was after every meal. I had to finish. If I didn't eat everything, I felt that I was wasting food.

Using guilt to get children to eat food is wrong. While some children may not pick up on the guilt-trip, others will. Somewhere along my childhood I picked up guilt around food and it has affected me beyond food. I am sure the 'children starving in Africa' remark at the dinner table is not a direct cause of my limiting belief that I should not have more than others, but I know it certainly didn't help.

The comfort

I recently saw a cookbook that was titled *Comfort Food*. It is commonly accepted that eating food can be comforting. This is another way parents use food against their children. 'Eat this, you will feel better.' Love is synonymous with food. No wonder your grandmother tried to 'feed you up' or loved to treat you. It is their way of showing you that they love you.

However, doing this is a recipe for disaster. There has been many a movie about how a girl gets dumped by her boyfriend and comforts herself by eating a tub of ice-cream (*Bridget Jones's Diary*, anyone?). Or even the scene where someone suffers heartbreak so they hide in their apartment drinking litres of Coke and eating mountains of crap food (*Forgetting Sarah Marshall*, anyone?). You may even have experienced the opposite: falling in love and for some reason you drop a dress or trouser size. It seems love has been your food and you haven't needed any 'comfort' food to cheer you up.

As parents we can offer comfort through food in many ways, even as a form of distraction.

My good friend told me a story, of which I am sure you will have heard a variation. She was at a child's first birthday party. Out of the corner of her eye she spotted an 18-month-old fall over a toy. While the father rushed to pick this child up to stop her wailing, the mother went and got a cupcake and shoved it in the child's mouth to stop her crying. Then, without acknowledging that she may be hurt, they focused all their attention on that cupcake and how good it was. This story highlights how food is used to distract and nurture children. It is so easy to use food as a form of comfort through distraction, but what is this teaching children?

I grew up in a small town. We would drive 50 minutes to the nearest large supermarket to do our grocery shopping once a month. Whenever we got into the car we would get something to eat, no matter if we had just eaten or not. On most occasions it was lollies from the gas station. My favourite was raspberry drops and my mum's was heart chews. It was a tradition: we ate in the car. It was a way to distract us from the long journey ahead.

Fast-forward 20 years and I find it hard not to use food as a distraction in the car for my children and myself. Whenever I get into the car, especially for a road trip, I will pack food, just in case I get hungry. However, hungry or not I will eat whatever I have packed! It is not too much of an issue for me now, but when I worked two hours' drive away from home three days a week, the amount I ate increased significantly.

I have a ton of stories of how people use food for comfort that I could share with you, but chances are you probably have your own. Think about how and when you use food for comfort. Then think about the ways you may be setting your children up to use food for comfort.

ACTION STEPS

1. Write down a few examples in your own parenting when you have been:
   - authoritative (coaching)
   - authoritarian
   - permissive
   - neglectful
2. In what way do you use food as a reward, comfort or punishment or do you guilt-trip your children into eating food?
3. Do your children have an unnatural love of 'treat' food, lollies, chips, etc?
4. Do you treat unhealthy food as a reward, or show that it is something to be loved in your tone of voice?
5. How do you use food with your children?
6. What healthy foods do your children not like? Is this the same food you have used to bribe, punish or guilt-trip your children into eating?

ENCOURAGING CHILDREN TO EAT

It is not just what you say, but the way you say it and the meaning behind what you say. I remember when my youngest daughter, Eckhart, was in a big exploration stage. At her nana's house there are all sorts of cupboards to get into and explore. Some cupboards have a lot of breakables in them. One day when she was about to open one of these cupboards, her Poppa said, 'Out of there, Eckhart'. The tone he used was direct and a little bit harsh. I knew he wasn't grumpy, but Eckhart didn't. Her face screwed up and she burst into tears. He didn't mean to scare her, he just didn't want anything to get broken. A bit later in the day she went to the same cupboard and her Poppa adjusted his tone. In a higher pitch he again said, 'Out of there, Eckhart'. This time she didn't burst into tears, but looked at him for more guidance.

Children are not only interpreting our words but the meaning behind the words. 'Just one bite' and 'you will get used to it' are popular words of encouragement used at the dinner table, yet they can take on different meanings depending on how they are said.

I am a big fan of using 'just one bite', because children may need to try something 10–15 times before they develop a taste preference for it.[11] By getting children to take just one bite they develop the habit of trying new food, and also train their taste buds to the new taste (more on this later). This is the reason I like to say 'just one bite'.

I have lost sight of the woods for the trees at times and tried to enforce 'just one bite' a little too much. I have, at times, got so wrapped up in the fact that if they didn't have just one bite they would not get their taste buds used to the food, that I have forgotten it is the enjoyment of eating healthy food that will lead to enjoying tasting new foods and ultimately instilling healthy eating habits. I remember a few occasions where one or more of my children has not been in a great mood to try new food. I have been stubborn and forceful in the way I have said 'just one bite'. This has always backfired. They have met my stubborn authoritarian tone with even more stubbornness themselves. The dinner-time experience has become unhappy. Stand-offs, unhappiness, unadventurousness — not habits that I am wanting to instil in them.

I was out to dinner with some friends. Sarah had a two-year-old at the time, so she decided to order the chicken meal and share this with her daughter. Putting some of her meal onto a side plate, she included a little bit of everything, including the peas. He daughter popped a pea in her mouth, then proceeded to screw up her face, as if she had just eaten a lemon. We all had a slight giggle. When she said, 'Mummy, don't like', Sarah said, 'Don't worry, you will get used to it

— vegetables are good for you.' It was said in a way that implied 'Oh honey, I know, no one likes peas but they just eat them because they are good for them.' Compare this to another parent who says, 'You will get used to it, you just need to try it a few more times' in an upbeat tone. Only a slight variation on what is said and in a different tone, but the message behind the words is entirely different. The latter phrase implies a message of 'Vegetables taste good, you just need to practise eating them and become like an adult': a positive message.

Dinner time or war zone?

Dinner times are quite often when wars begin. All you want is for your children to eat some healthy food, and this may be your only chance for the day to get them to eat some vegetables, just so you are satisfied that they are getting enough nutrients. How do you encourage your children to eat? I have asked many people how their parents encouraged them to eat or how they encourage their children to eat at dinner times. The most common answers are:

1. You cannot leave until you eat everything on your plate.
2. You must eat all your dinner and then you will get dessert.
3. Eat some more — think about all those starving people in Africa.
4. You will get used to the taste.

The words you use to encourage your children to eat can have hidden messages. Not all children who have been raised with these words will have received the same message. We all interpret the world differently. One child can take offence and shut down if an adult says, 'You made a mistake', and another child sees those words as a chance to learn and will keep trying until they get it right. Let's look at the words so often used at dinner times to encourage children to eat, and see how they could affect people's relationship with food.

1. You cannot leave until you eat everything on your plate

I remember hiding food that I really didn't want to eat under my bottom so that I created the illusion that I had finished everything on my plate. I have heard other stories of feeding the dog or 'giving' food to their younger sibling who wasn't looking, just so the person could get through the 'finish everything on your plate' issue. 'Finishing everything on your plate' encourages children to do so even when they are not enjoying the food they are eating. I know a lot of people who feel they have to finish everything on their plate without question. These same people will exclaim, 'Come on, Wal, you cannot leave that little bit', when I now leave some food on my plate. I almost feel obliged to eat it to satisfy them! It encourages eating for eating's sake and then developing an uncomfortably full tummy.

The consequence: Many consequences can come from instilling a 'you must clean your plate' habit, from weight gain to not having the ability to self-regulate food intake. I was encouraged to finish everything on my plate when growing up. It was a habit I grew into and a habit I continued, even after leaving my parents' home. Even if I wanted to, I couldn't stop eating until all the food was gone. This was disastrous for me in my late teens and early twenties. I had high anxiety levels as it was, and eating to an uncomfortable level of fullness just exacerbated this. The only relief I had was to throw up my dinner.

As I said earlier, I developed bulimia because I thought I had to have something wrong with me. Overeating and cleaning my plate was a trigger for me. Vomiting became a habit. I threw up about 60 per cent of my evening meals for about seven years. The uncomfortable fullness was my trigger. Even now, when on odd occasions I overeat to the point of feeling uncomfortably full, I have to remind myself that I have a choice not to throw up! Throwing up is something I haven't done in over 10 years, but it is still a part of my default setting when I feel uncomfortably full, as I know it will take away the uncomfortable sensation of overeating.

While another person will have a different experience from being told to eat everything on their plate, this was my experience. In chapter six we will look at ways you can help your children develop internal cues so they do not get to the uncomfortably full stage.

2. *You must eat all your dinner and then you will get dessert*

These words are very encouraging and seem so innocent. They are used not only at the dinner table but, as we saw previously, as a source of reward: 'Be good and then you will get a treat.' Oh, the bribe. I can hear voices now: if I cannot bribe my children how will I get them to behave, how will they do what I want them to do? (Keep reading, this will be addressed in upcoming chapters.)

Although I cannot remember these words being used so much when I was little, I know they were present. How do I know? Because it has been my go-to. Also, I hear my parents and family members say these words when encouraging their grandchildren to eat their vegetables. The number of times I have bribed my children with some sort of food is hard to admit. To this day I have to consciously stop mid-sentence, 'If you're good, I'll . . .' Although it has been dried mango or some other healthy alternative, it is still a bribe with food and ultimately has the same consequence.

The consequence: Food becomes a reward, a part of an emotional eating pattern. So many people think they struggle with willpower over food when most of the time it is not about willpower, but more about rewarding themselves.

3. *Eat some more — think about all those starving people in Africa*

While I have covered how guilt can affect your relationship with food, I want to tell you another story about it.

Pete, a client, had a prime case of guilt about food. Like Pavlov's dog, he would associate eating with guilt. Whenever Pete felt guilty about something in his life, he would turn to food. It was a trigger for him to eat, even though he was not hungry. He could not help it. When talking about his childhood experiences at the dinner table, he said that his mother was aloof at dinner times, yet there was a constant feeling of guilt. He had to eat all his dinner to please his mother. The only thing his mother would say was 'Africa': one word to remind him of all those starving people. He then associated this guilt-trip with eating, right into his adult life.

The consequence: Guilt around food can be an association to use food when you feel guilty, and also becomes an emotional attachment to food.

4. You will get used to the taste

This is more ambiguous. The tone used to say this is more important than the actual words. Children's taste buds are *formed* not found out.[12] Children learn to like and dislike food. However, when someone uses the words 'Don't worry, you will get used to the taste', it can imply 'Yep, it is disgusting, but you will be soon be desensitised to it'. The clincher, though, is that it is often used for vegetables. When a child doesn't like something that is unhealthy, like ice-cream, it is often met with amazement and 'Really? Try it again — are you sure you don't like it?'

The consequence: A few years ago we had a few friends stay with us. It was summer and I was right into making different salads and eating more raw food. I had made a salad that had raw cauliflower in it. My friend was devouring this salad. Midway through, he stabbed a piece of cauliflower, held it up and innocently asked, 'What is this?' It was covered in a homemade cashew-avocado dressing that disguised the shape of it. When I replied 'cauliflower' he almost fell off his chair. The conversation turned to how as an adult he ate healthy food only because he thought he 'had to'. He didn't really enjoy the taste of most healthy food, but had got used to the taste. His childhood memory of dinner times was tender, but he had a distinct memory of eating vegetables he didn't like and his father saying, 'Don't worry, son, you will get used to it' — like it was a badge of honour that responsible adults wore. While this is a story that didn't have too disastrous effects on this friend, others have told me how they either went through a phase of rebelling, or even still rebel, against all things healthy, because they taste horrible. They have a belief that healthy food cannot taste good. Period.

ACTION STEPS

The words and phrases you use to encourage your children to eat at dinner times will influence whether your children will willingly try and accept new food.

1. Reflect on the words your parents used at dinner times to encourage you to eat your vegetables. How has this impacted on your relationship with food? On how you parent?
2. What words do you use to encourage your children to eat more of the healthy stuff at dinner times? What messages could they take from these seemingly encouraging words?

CAUSING FIGHTS

If you want to cause fights with your children, if you want to create unhappy mealtimes, or if you just want to have children who turn into adults who do the opposite of everything that you've taught them, then do these two things: restrict food and control their eating.

Restrictiveness

When a food is restricted, it is wanted more. Fisher and Birch,[13] two of the top researchers in this area, found that when a particular food was restricted, this food got more positive comments and more requests than when the same food was made freely available. The children also took larger portions and ate more of the restricted food (when the restrictions were lifted) compared to when the same food was always freely accessible.

This is not rocket science. It is human nature. When someone says 'No' to something, we will want it even more. It is called the scarcity principle.

Researchers wanted to know how people value cookies. In one jar they put 10 cookies, in another, identical jar they placed two of the same cookies. Participants in this study considered the cookies in the jar with only two cookies as more valuable. Scarcity somehow affected their perception of value.[14]

I don't think of myself as a sucker, but just the other day I was lured in. I was considering buying an informational product. I was umming and aahing over it and wasn't quite sure. Then came the email. You have probably had the same email or some version of it: 'Buy now and get it at a reduced price', 'Offer ends this Friday' or 'Only a few spots left'. 'Only a few spots left' got me. Bang, before you could say 'Bob's your uncle' I had purchased this product. I didn't want to miss out, after all! Scarcity is a time-tested marketing technique that works; I am sure you have been affected by it in some way. Food is no different.

When food is made scarce or it is restricted, you want it more and you want it now. When I was little I sneaked food. I could sniff out chocolate a mile away, and, in fact, I would often walk that mile to get the chocolate. Our grandfather, who lived at the bottom of the hill about a mile from our house, always had fruit and nut chocolate in his fridge. My sisters and I would find the unlocked window, sneak in and eat it — most of it. We would be polite and leave a few squares. I sneaked it because we were never given chocolate and it was something that adults ate freely. The weird thing is, I never liked fruit and nut chocolate that much. I loved it when my grandfather had milk chocolate, but even though I didn't like fruit and nut, I ate it anyway. Who knew when I was going to get some more chocolate?

As adults, sneaking food may not be a regular occurrence (unless you are at your parents' house again and you revert back to your childhood ways), but it still happens. I was in the supermarket one day, rushing around and about to go to the checkout lane. As I came around a corner I startled a lady who was putting chocolate in her trolley. She looked at me very sheepishly and said, 'You caught me'. I was taken by surprise, as she was just putting chocolate into her trolley, but I could see that she felt guilty about having something she 'knew' she shouldn't have.

Deprivation diets don't work, never have. Diets where you have to restrict calories or some type of food, like bread, can work in the short term, but more often than not the weight is piled back on when the restrictions are lifted.

What happens when your children go out into the big wide world and they don't have you there to restrict their access to food? They will do the same as dieters: they will eat more.

When you deprive yourself of something, you crave it more and more. Children are no different; in fact, they are arguably worse off, because they do not have the knowledge we do about healthy and unhealthy food and its effects on our bodies.

Control

Why do we tow a trailer? Why not push it? If we tried to push it we would realise that it could end up anywhere, yet when we lead it, it will always end up where we want it to go. (Unless it is on ice, that is, then it is a wild guess where it ends up!)

When we try to control our children in anything, eating included, it is a bit of an unknown where they will end up. Controlling food intake is attempted through many different avenues (see page 81). Ah gosh, it works. It's easy, so effective and so innocent. However, the long-term effect is anything but innocent. By controlling your children's diet, they are not given the opportunity to learn through experience. Your children's food intake is then disrupted and fewer fruit and vegetables are eaten, and in some cases the long-term preference for those vegetables is decreased.

I had a belief that my children would not like spinach, so I never served it to them. When I started to question how my beliefs affected my children, I started to put it on their plate. For the first few times, I put it on their plate and said nothing. Sometimes when preparing dinner I would talk about how I was looking forward to eating the meal that night as I really felt like some spinach. After a few times, when the food was no longer 'new' to them, Rasmus commented that he didn't like it. When I asked if he had tried it, he looked confused.

I took my chance. I explained the story of Popeye and how, when he ate spinach, he would sprout muscles and become stronger. I even sang him a song. Then I 'thought' out loud, 'I wonder if that is why Dad is so strong?' I could see the cogs in his head turning. Dad was the strongest man Rasmus knew, and he ate and loved spinach. I never once mentioned that Rasmus himself would become stronger by eating it or encouraged him to eat it, we just talked around it. Quite honestly I didn't expect him to try it. But after the conversation had turned to something else, he turned to me and said he liked spinach. All his spinach had disappeared! He ate the spinach on his terms, no nagging or forcing on my part. He developed a positive association with spinach, something that he will always have.

The opposite of this is controlling what your children eat or forcing them to eat certain foods. Sure they may eat it then, but the associations formed are negative.

I was at my parents for dinner with my sister. When my mother asked if we wanted any peas, my sister replied that she doesn't like peas because 'you forced them on me when I was little'. Like I said earlier, I also remember her being forced to eat her peas. I am the youngest, so by the time it was my turn to learn about vegetables and eating, my parents seemed to enforce eating vegetables less. They had learnt it not only didn't work, but also made the dinner-table experience awful.

It is a common practice for parents to restrict access to 'forbidden' food and control their children's diets through bribes, rewards, punishment or even guilt. It is easy to talk about and show you the reasons why this is not good. You may even be sitting down now and thinking 'Yeah, those parents who do that . . .', judging them for doing such things to their children.

The more I have talked with parents about these practices the more I see, even if someone is very restrictive in what they give their children to eat, they are doing it because they ultimately love their kids. They want the best for them. Controlling and restricting food is just what they know. It is the way they have been taught to encourage their children to eat healthy food.

OKAY, BUT NOW WHAT?

You may now be thinking 'This is all good, but how do I trust my children to eat healthy food without using restrictiveness or control?' Hold your horses, in the next few chapters it will become clear. For now, I want you to be aware of the possible lessons you will teach your children when you force food on them or restrict food. Concentrate on coaching habits, long-term habits.

The next chapters are all about how to coach children. We need to get away from the nutritional mindset of *feeding* our children certain foods because they will get *x* amount of protein or other nutrients that seem to be in vogue. Start thinking about nutrition as a habit. What eating habits do you want to instil in your children?

ACTION STEPS

1. Did you grow up with food restriction or control?
2. Have you been restricting or controlling food for your children?
3. What other ways could you encourage your children to eat better? (We will look a lot at this in the upcoming steps, but for now I want you to try to think about it differently for yourself.)

CHAPTER FOUR

WHERE TO START

This chapter is critical, as it will help you to get clear in your head how you want to teach your children about food. Instead of teaching your children by default, you can actively think about what you say about and do with individual foods as well as around mealtimes, and how this implants ideas in your children's evolving minds. I will also introduce you to the idea of 'food levels', while keeping food neutral. Children need consistency, and by you developing clear ideas about levels of food, you can parent accordingly.

PUTTING FOOD ON A PEDESTAL

Parents do it

'Mummy, Mummy — Grandma gave me some candy.' How would you react to your child saying this? Along with many parents, I have reacted by saying the word 'Lucky!' in a drawn-out tone. Even if you are not pleased with your mother or mother-in-law for giving your children sweets, your child seems so pleased with themselves you feel you cannot rain on their parade.

Words and phrases like 'lucky' and 'who's been a good girl, then' are commonplace around children and unhealthy food. We are led to believe that children (our past selves included) love sweet, fried and generally unhealthy food. We then teach them, inadvertently, of course, what they should like and shouldn't like. We do this through words we use either directly, like 'lucky' when referring to getting treats, or in throwaway comments such as 'sorry, there is no kid food here', when looking at a table with a huge selection of foods.

When I was writing this book I was visiting my wider family. I had become hyper-aware of comments around food, both with family and visiting friends. At one family lunch, I counted five comments in an hour from one person who was in earshot of my children, such as 'Oh, they won't like that' and 'There is no food good for children here', when referring to the lovely ham, salmon and salad put out to eat, as well as 'You're lucky' and 'How come you got that?' when referring to ice-cream and dessert.

These are seemingly innocent remarks; however, they enforce an idea, a belief. A belief that children don't like and won't eat the foods adults eat, like vegetables. A belief that they prefer sweets and dessert-type food. A belief that you probably share — not necessarily because it is true but because it was taught to you when your brain was at an impressionable stage.

Tommy was a friend's son, aged five. He only ate white and beige food. Anything with colour seemed to repulse him. Tommy's mum was worried that he would not try any food that even had a slight bit of colour in it. I watched as she talked about her son's eating habits to other parents. Some parents responded by helping to justify Tommy's behaviour, saying, 'Oh, but what kid does?' Others offered advice: 'No child likes vegetables, you just need to hide them'. All the while Tommy was sitting in his mother's lap.

This scene, or some version of it, is not uncommon: a parent worried that their children are not eating what the other children eat and other parents trying to help, either by justifying or encouraging that parent with similar words to the ones used above. I am sure you have even been a part of one of these conversations. Put yourself in Tommy's shoes. What does he hear? 'Children don't like vegetables.' 'Vegetables are not nice to eat.' 'Who likes vegetables?' These words teach or, in Tommy's case, reinforce that vegetables or colourful food are not for children. They are foods that are not nice to eat and are only eaten by adults because it is good for them.

Society does it

Unfortunately, food is also portrayed positively (sweets) and negatively (vegetables) outside of your home. As your children will not be with you all the time they will get exposed to these messages. When they go to school or preschool, they will get messages from other children — what is cool and uncool. Food is not immune. The way society views food, what is thought of as being nice to eat and what is yucky, will influence them in some way.

Colour the food you love . . .

Colour the food you hate . . .

The pictures on the previous page are similar to those in many of my children's activity books. Children are always asked to draw or colour in the food they love or the food they hate or think is 'yuck'. This might seem innocent enough, but looking at the pictures in more detail you will see that the foods they are encouraged to colour in because they love them are mostly candies, chips or some other junk food. The foods they are encouraged to colour in because they don't like them are mostly vegetables, fish or 'real foods'. This is reinforcing the belief that a child should love bright-coloured sweets and loathe green food such as vegetables.

This doesn't just happen in activity books: movies, TV, anything and everything aimed at children has some sort of reinforcement of this idea. Huxley recently watched the children's movie called *Inside Out*. In this movie there are characters based on the emotions a person experiences, including sadness, joy, anger, fear and disgust. I began asking her what each emotion was. When it was disgust's turn, she said, 'Like when you get given broccoli, disgust comes out.' It turns out that in this movie there is a scene where the main character was given broccoli for the first time. Disgust grabbed hold of the controls in her head so that she would not try it. Again it might seem very innocent, yet why is this always done with vegetables — why not lollies? We are literally teaching children they should find vegetables disgusting!

Most treats given to children are forms of sugar. I was shopping with Rasmus one afternoon and as I passed by a clothing store a lady came running out and gave him two lollies. Why don't we give carrots? A few months earlier Rasmus and I had gone on a farm visit with his preschool and all the children were given carrots at the end. Although I cannot say which one he liked better, he did ask for seconds of those delicious farm-fresh carrots, but not of the lollies.

If you have ever taken your children on a plane you will have likely been asked if your children would like to have a children's meal. I mistakenly said yes on one trip. Airplane food can be a bit iffy anyway, but the children's meals served were terrible. It's like someone said, 'Okay, we are serving children. Don't put in anything with colour and make sure it has as much sugar in it as possible.'

It is a belief system in our society that children do not like healthy food, that broccoli is 'disgusting' and sweets are a 'treat'. As I see it, we have two options: one is to say, 'Well, that is how it is, we are not going to change society and I cannot do anything.' The other option is to realise that as a parent you get to influence what your children are exposed to. Failing that, you get to talk to your children in a way that will encourage a healthier relationship with food. As parents we can flip this switch.

We pick up some of our beliefs not necessarily because they are what we have chosen to believe in, but because the majority of people believe it. Most people want to fit in, so when a majority believes in something we fall in behind. (Except you, that is — that is why you are reading this book!) Yet it is still hard to escape. Society's norms and pressures have influenced your relationship with food and will influence your children's if you are not aware of it. However, by becoming aware of it, you can minimise the impact that it has on your children.

Advertising does it

Advertising affects what food we buy and what our children eat and even want to eat. Dr Kiyah Duffey wrote that the 2006 Institute of Medicine report concluded that there was substantial evidence that 'food and beverage marketing influences the preference and purchase requests of children'.[15] Primary school-aged children ate 45 per cent more snack food after watching programmes containing food advertising compared to children who watched the same programmes without food advertising.

I am reminded of one of my lectures at university. We watched a documentary that followed a team of researchers who wanted to see how far they could push the advertising and food labelling laws. They made a fruit mousse that consisted of sugar and fruit flavouring with some added nutrients, and marketed it as a healthy yoghurt treat. They packaged the 'yoghurt' in bright colours that attracted children and they used words to suggest it was a 'healthy choice' for parents to choose for their kids. They then made a TV advertisement that made it look cool for the children, and suggested it was healthy (for parents, of course). Hidden cameras caught children begging their parents to buy this 'healthy snack' and the parents looking at it a little and then putting it in their shopping basket.

After they had put it in their trolleys, the parents were interviewed by the researchers and asked what their motivation was behind buying that food item. While some admitted it was because their children had asked for it, most said it was because they believed it was a healthy snack. These parents genuinely thought they were buying their children a healthy yoghurt snack and not a fruit mousse that was over 70 per cent sugar.

Before you dismiss this by thinking that they must have been unhealthy parents, they were all normal-weight, healthy-looking adults. Go and look at the 'kid food' you have in your fridge and pantry and see how much sugar, colourings and additives are in there before you judge! The bottom line is, advertising works.

All is not lost

It is normal to put unhealthy food on a pedestal and healthy food in the should-do pile. These are messages that your children are getting bombarded with on a daily basis. I encourage you to think about how you label food and the comments you use around food. Are you maybe unknowingly teaching your children that healthy food is not nice to eat and that sweets are treats and therefore more desirable?

Our beliefs are shaped by our parents, society and advertising. At this point you may be thinking 'Okay, I can help my children to have a healthy relationship with food through what I do, but I cannot change what they will learn from society and advertising.' Or you may be thinking of the steps you could put in place to shelter your children from such influences. Either way, don't be a negative Nelly. Just being aware of these external influences can help you consciously parent to combat these pressures.

Advertising and society's views are not going to change or go away overnight. The way I see it, you can either complain about it or use it to your advantage. Coach children to become aware of what is affecting their food choices. When they ask for that brightly coloured yoghurt treat, coach them to be aware by asking why they would like to try it. Show them how advertising is encouraging them to buy things by using bright colours, etc.

We will go through this more in upcoming chapters, but for now just know that although they may not comprehend exactly what you are saying straight away, the more you draw attention to these influences, the more they will become aware of how advertising and other people's views affect them. Encourage them to be an individual and think for themselves. This, combined with chapter six's 'Checking-in', will go a long way to creating children who rarely make food decisions based on external cues like advertising.

ACTION STEPS

1. What food do you put on a pedestal by teaching your children that it is a treat, or rewarding them with it?
2. What language do you use to reinforce that unhealthy food tastes good?
3. Over the next week, observe the messages that your children are receiving about food from TV, media, books and other adults.

WHAT FOOD MEANS TO YOU

Mealtimes

Mealtimes, especially dinner times, can have a major influence on how your children perceive food. You set the tone. When you think of dinner times, do you get anxious and apprehensive at the thought of tantrums and battles of control? What do you remember from eating dinner with your family? Perhaps you didn't eat with your parents? What feelings and emotions are conjured up just by thinking about your mealtime experiences as a child?

Some of you will get defensive at this question: 'I want to learn to be a parent to my children, not conjure up my childhood experiences.' While I agree with moving forward, and not getting stuck in the past with the old line of 'oh, my parents were terrible', to move forward and expand on the lessons our parents taught us, we need to shed light on our beliefs and habits. We need to become aware. This awareness can help you to see your parents' relationship with food and the messages behind your interactions.

I was fortunate to grow up with very loving parents. They raised me on healthy, fresh farm food. We didn't have an abundance of money but we always had good food to eat. My dinner times were spent around the table with the family. I have hazy memories, but I do remember the TV being on periodically. We were expected to 'clean our plates', at times even finishing all the peas, even though my older sister physically gagged on them. When I didn't feel like eating much, I was told that we should, because there were people starving in Africa. We were told we should feel grateful. Sometimes if we finished everything on our plate we got a treat of ice-cream or some sweet-filled dessert. That was our reward for eating mushy greens.

At this point, I want to say I am not 'getting at' my parents. We instinctively parent on what we have learnt in our past and hope we can prepare our children for the future. I am very grateful to my parents and what they taught me about food. My dad's parents would physically shove silver beet down his throat so that he would eat what he 'should' eat. (Needless to say, he still doesn't eat silver beet and I also have an aversion to it!) I am grateful that he had the capacity to change his parenting style from what he had grown up with. Trying to parent 'better' than we were parented as children is a part of human evolution. It's how we evolve as a society. I know my children will do the same!

I recently had the pleasure of helping a young teen, Lucy, to eat better. Lucy and her mum initially came to me together. When I asked about their dinner-table experiences, her mum said, 'Oh, she eats in her room. She doesn't want to have dinner with her parents!' It was said with a tone that implied that she accepted that Lucy thought it was 'uncool' to eat with her parents. She was a teenager, after all! However, when Lucy and I had some time alone at a later point, I asked her about eating dinner in her room. She replied that she did so because 'my parents don't want to eat with me'. They both thought they were doing each other a favour, Lucy by eating in her room and her mother by letting it slide. Lucy felt her parents didn't care enough about her to let her eat with them.

I knew Lucy's mum thought she was being caring by letting Lucy eat in her room. However, I was intrigued at how it got to be this way. I found that, when Lucy was young, her mother and father would have their meal and Lucy would have hers separately. Lucy had her food, which was served earlier, and once she was in bed, her parents would have 'their time' and have their meal together. Adult food and adult time for them, and time with Lucy was treated as separate — so it was 'kid food' for her.

What messages do you think Lucy was getting here? Think about going into your parents' house now, or even over to a friend's house for dinner. Imagine the cook busy in the kitchen, with the smell of your favourite food wafting into your olfactory senses. The plate gets dished up and handed to you: 'Here's your dinner. The rest of us will eat later.' I don't know about you, but I get feelings of smallness and insignificance. I wouldn't feel respected. While the feelings will differ for everyone, there is likely to be a sense of rejection. Unless you are a complete introvert and relish not having to make conversation over the dinner table! Children are the same. Children are little humans. They have all the same feelings and emotions as adults do, only they have not learnt to comprehend or put words to these feelings and emotions. I think it is a great idea to eat with your children, but I know that some people's lives cannot accommodate this for one reason or another. If this is you, then talk to your children about it. Some children are more sensitive than others, and the extent to which you make a conversation about it will depend on your child.

The way you see mealtimes will indirectly influence what your children associate with food. Make it fun, make it positive. In chapter seven we will go into more detail about the practicalities of making mealtimes fun and full of positive associations.

Cooking

Christina was a parent who found preparing food and cooking to be the worst part of her day. She hated it. To compound it, her children were picky eaters. Her words were, 'They are a nightmare at dinner times.' It was obvious that her energy showed them 'this is a hassle for me'. It was easier for her to get snack food and let the children eat it by themselves. Although she was more of a coaching parent in other areas, when it came to food she was very permissive. Food was a stress factor for her as a parent, and she provided her children with no boundaries.

As we talked some more, she said that she didn't think she was a good cook, so why try? On the occasions when she had put effort into her cooking, her children didn't like it and were ungrateful.

I have also had similar feelings. When you try your best to put good food on the table after a long day, then are met with 'I don't like it', in a voice with a slight sneer and drawn-out tone, it is difficult not to get snarky and say, 'Well, go hungry then', in the same tone. As it turned out, for Christina it wasn't that she didn't like to cook, she just felt that she wasn't a good cook, so why make the effort?

In *Mindless Eating*, American researcher Brian Wansink defines a good cook as someone who:

1. buys different food
2. tries new recipes
3. substitutes different ingredients into favourite recipes
4. takes children to the grocery store and lets them choose a new healthy food
5. visits authentic ethnic restaurants.

I loved these five points. When I told Christina about them, she realised that she didn't need to be the world's best cook, that just trying new food and cooking new meals was good enough. She relaxed. Her expectation of her own cooking dropped and she experienced a different energy when she cooked and served food to her children.

Labels

Words are powerful. Yet often people say things without thinking. When my eldest daughter was about 14 months old, she went through a shy stage. She had been a child who would go to anyone and was good with new people, but during this phase she would cling onto my legs and try to hide when adults asked her questions or even simply said 'Hello'. I found myself saying, 'Oh, she is just shy.'

As parents we all have ideals of what we want for our children. When our children don't meet these ideals, we justify them with words such as 'She is just shy', 'He is a show-off', 'It takes a while for her to warm up'. Ben and I, being new parents, were no different. 'She is just shy' was spoken a lot over a few weeks and we noticed Huxley becoming less and less interested in new people. She even started to shy away from good friends that she would see most. We had an idea that us saying the phrase 'she is just shy' consistently reinforced this shyness and she then took it on as her identity. I guess this was a way of living up to our expectations.

We decided that we would not label her as 'shy', and if someone asked, 'Oh, is she shy?', our reply would be 'No'. No explanation, no justification for why she was hiding between our legs. It caught a few people by surprise, as she was clearly being shy, but we chose not to label her with those words. It only took a few days of taking the 'she is just shy' out of what we said and she was back to welcoming in friends with hugs and strangers with eye contact.

This is not the only time we have done this. My son, Rasmus, was born in Japan. When we lived there, we didn't have a car. When we returned to New Zealand on a holiday when he was 14 months old, he was strapped into a car seat for the first time. We were also travelling around the country visiting friends, so the hours strapped into the car were a shock for him.

He was a terrible traveller. Driving was not a happy experience for him or us. Having so much success with not labelling Huxley, we decided to see if reinforcing an idea would work. Ben and I constantly spoke about what good travellers both Rasmus and his sister were. When our friends asked, 'How was the trip?', we would respond, 'Great. The children are good travellers.' I thought we were overdoing it, yet, although he was only 14 months, Rasmus got it. He was far from perfect, but he stopped throwing an absolute fit when he was being strapped into the car seat. He gradually took longer to get to the point of losing it when we were driving.

The point is that your words, even said innocently, both positive and negative, will rub off on your children. The words you use generally around food, especially if you are trying to encourage your children to eat better, influence what they eat or don't eat. If you have labelled your children as bad eaters, then stop. You don't need to say something that is not true if that doesn't suit you, but stop labelling them. Keep the words you use to describe your children's eating or relationship with food neutral.

How *you* see mealtimes, cooking and your children, and what you bring to the table (pun intended), will influence your children. Just like my swimming coach saw my leanness through his beliefs, you can also see food experiences through your beliefs.

ACTION STEPS

1. What is the tone at mealtimes in your house? Is it happy and peaceful or is it full of tension, stand-offs, etc?
2. Do you resent cooking and preparing meals? How does this affect your children?
3. Do you label your children as bad eaters or as not liking certain foods? What other ways do you reinforce these labels?

START WITH YOURSELF

I am sure you have walked into a room where you felt tense or uncomfortable. We often feel things first and then look for reasons to back up what we feel, to justify our feelings. We walk into a room and feel the tension, then we look at the people in the room and look for a grumpy look or an angry glance. I know you are probably thinking of a situation when this has happened.

I have been in this situation many times. While travelling around with three children, visiting family and friends, I realised staying in their space can be challenging. However, I have learnt that, more often than not, it is not anger or grumpiness we see when we look around. Often that person is thinking about things they need to get done or something else that is going on in their lives. It is not that they are grumpy per se, but rather not 100 per cent present.

Even being in a relationship has been an eye-opener for me. When Ben and I were first married, he would come home from a challenging day of work and not be fully present. As he wasn't his normal self, I thought that he was grumpy, and often that he was grumpy with me. I would constantly ask him, 'Is there anything wrong?' To me he seemed to be putting out a grumpy feeling, while to him he was just thinking how he could have handled the day differently. Nothing to do with me or with being grumpy!

I have also seen the difference in my children when I am not fully present at dinner times. When I am distracted, because I am thinking about other things in my life, I am not fully present for them at the dinner table. My children can then 'act up' to get my attention, which in the past has been met with 'grumpy mum'. I have not had the capacity to be with them at the dinner table as well as think about something else.

If you have any anxiety around food due to your low body image or your expectations as a parent, you will likely have an energy at the dinner table that is not 100 per cent present. Children react to this and will either pick up on your anxiety and learn that this is the way to behave around food, or they may act up, thereby creating an undesirable dinner-table experience.

Your body image

If you have any anxiety around food, including any sort of eating disorder or obsessive compulsive disorder (OCD), then you need to read this section. The energy that you put out affects the way your children interact with food. The more anxiety you have the more anxiety your children will have and dinner will become a war zone. Whether it is your children learning 'through osmosis' or the way you parent your children because of your anxiety, it affects your children. Parents with some sort of anxiety towards food tend to have parenting practices in the authoritarian tone; they put more pressure or restrictions on their children and become more controlling of the type of food eaten and how it is eaten.

For example, the amount of pressure that Amanda was putting on Susie in the example in chapter one was obvious to me. Amanda felt she needed to control what her daughter ate because other parents were starting to talk about how skinny her child was. Susie met her mother with equal amounts of control. Amanda felt a lot of anxiety around food and her parenting style reflected these issues.

Thinking back to chapter two when we learnt about the developing brain, from day one children are looking to their parents or caregivers at mealtimes and 'downloading' how they should then act around food. If parents have high anxiety levels or are stressed out by their interactions with food, children will mirror this in their own behaviour. For children, they think this is how they should react around food. This is all they know and they will behave accordingly.

As a parent

Have you ever felt judged as a parent on what you give your children to eat? I am sure I am not alone in feeling this. I constantly felt that I could not get it right. When I restricted what I gave my children in the sweets department, I was met with remarks such as 'One lolly won't hurt them' or 'They are children, they love that food, don't deprive them.' When I gave them an ice-cream, I was met with comments such as 'I didn't think you would give them that.' I constantly felt judged at what I gave my children to eat.

When you have anxiety as a parent or you are overly concerned with how much, how little or what type of food your children are eating, you are more likely to parent with pressure and restriction, an authoritarian style of parenting. As we saw in chapter three this type of parenting promotes challenging eating behaviours and therefore creates an issue with eating.

Once parents who I meet socially know I am a nutritionist, they tend to react in one of two ways. They either start asking lots of questions or for advice, which I am always happy to chat about, or they start to push their children to eat more and put pressure on them to eat more vegetables or what they think is healthy. Sometimes in front of me they restrict or get their children to hide the unhealthy food they have already been given. I have been in many situations where parents justify their children's eating to me with, 'Oh, they normally love cucumber.' On some occasions when parents expect me to be watching how many vegetables their children eat, they will put more pressure on their children to eat, almost at times pleading with them or enforcing bribes to encourage them to eat. Without fail their children will not respond nicely to the pressure.

Here is a little secret: I personally don't look at what the child is eating, but I am intrigued by the way the parents interact with their children around food. When a parent gets to know me better as a friend, they realise that I am not judging them and they leave their children to it. And most, if not all, of the food will get eaten. When you provide a loving environment for your children and meet their requests or provide encouragement through warmth, you are fostering better eating practices. A few years ago I decided to do a little experiment. I noted down how I was feeling before I started preparing a meal: sad, angry, grumpy, stressed, happy, relaxed, playful — whatever words came to mind. I then cooked dinner, sat down and ate it, and once the children were in bed I would write down what happened at the dinner table: if the children were happy and contented, if they seemed to whine a lot or throw a tantrum, food-related or otherwise; just the general feel to the mealtime. There was a definite correlation between my feelings and the children's reactions.

Even if I was happy overall, but felt a little stressed, the children were more unsettled. The more I was present and happier within myself at the dinner table, the more I was able to meet their requests with warmth and understanding, the better they behaved and, more often than not, the more vegetables they ate without anything being said.

I encourage you to try this for yourself, because even though I knew this before I started this experiment, I thought it was too simple to make a difference. When I put effort into how I was feeling on the inside rather than watching and reacting to what my children were doing, I was really amazed at how much my energy affected the children.

The energy you have when serving food to your children, which affects your parenting style, affects your children's eating behaviours. If your dinner-table experiences are more unhappy than happy, first look to yourself. How can you make the energy of the dinner table in your house more positive? Perhaps it is relooking at your habits and how you see food, or perhaps it is re-evaluating your expectations of your children or your cooking. The person who cooks defines the majority of the mealtime experience. Make it fun.

ACTION STEPS

1. How does your energy affect your children at mealtimes?
2. Does this energy change depending on what company you are in? If so, how does this flow on to your children?
3. Do you have any anxiety around food? Are your children picking up on this? Do you put more pressure on your children because of this anxiety?

Note: Talk about this with the person who knows you best. Sometimes we cannot see how our energy affects the people around us. If you do notice your energy getting in the way of happy mealtimes, know that you're not alone and be grateful that you can see this — this is the first step in change, or going forward.

KEEP FOOD NEUTRAL

While reading this, you have probably been thinking, 'How do I actually teach my children about food or get them to eat if I cannot bribe them with food?' If I don't say, 'Eat your vegetables before you get dessert', how do I get them to eat their veges?

While we will discuss this further in the upcoming chapters, for now I want you to add to this: I want you to keep food neutral. By keeping food, no matter whether it is ice-cream or broccoli, neutral, our children's emotional attachment to food decreases and the capacity to try new (healthy) food also increases. A conundrum, I know, but true nonetheless. When we, as parents, have an agenda that children should eat a certain type or amount of food, we are more likely to put pressure on them. And pressure is a recipe for disaster.

Ben told me a story about when he was at school. He woke up one morning, planning to go for a run and then spend the rest of the day preparing for an upcoming exam for one of his favourite subjects. He came back from his run at about 10.30am and sat down for some breakfast. Just as he was finishing eating, and looking forward to studying, his mum walked in. She asked if he had studied that morning. When he said, 'I am about to', she said something like, 'Good. You need to pass these exams if...' To someone else this might have looked like words of encouragement. To Ben it felt like pressure. Even though he had been looking forward to studying, he decided that he was going to do the opposite of what his mum expected. I am sure you have your version of how your parents put pressure on you, and even though you wanted to do what they were saying to do, you rebelled. You did it on principle.

Serving food and encouraging children to eat is no different. Once we put pressure on children, their autonomy goes out the door. If they don't rebel in that instance they will rebel later on in life. Resist putting pressure on your children and instead talk about new food, so it doesn't feel 'new'. Talk about how you love it, how you used to think that this meal or vegetable tasted horrible and how you were surprised to find that it did taste good. Take the pressure off when serving food and you will find your children are more likely to eat more of the healthy stuff.

How do you take the pressure off? Keep in mind that all food is neutral. Don't overemphasise one food and treat it above other food. By keeping food neutral you are coaching your children to form autonomy around food. Instead, think about food in levels.

FOOD LEVELS

There are many ways of classing food, from macronutrients such as proteins to fats to glycaemic index and glycaemic load. Governments use food pyramids and 'My Plate'-type diagrams to classify food, and Weightwatchers uses points. This has always bugged me. Even when learning about this at university I could not quite comprehend it.

I like things to be practical, and counting calories and adding up the estimated amount of calcium in my food to make sure I was getting enough was tedious for me. And I am passionate about health! However, I also know people like to have a guide. This is where food groups come in.

Food groups are just that: groups of foods. While this is not a new concept, I think we should keep the labelling of these groups neutral. If we call processed food 'treat food' I think we are setting children up for thinking less of 'real food'. Real food can be treat food as well!

I suggest grouping food into the following levels:

- **Real food/alive food**: food that has been grown and picked and that is eaten in this form — fresh and healthy. Includes vegetables, fruit, nuts, unprocessed meats, etc. These foods are encouraged to be eaten first.
- **Now-and-again food**: food that is often classed as healthy. The level of processing is minimal. Includes bread, yoghurt, pasta, home baking, etc. These foods are fine to have on an everyday basis; however, they should be eaten with or after real foods.
- **Processed food**: food that is heavily processed. This food often has added sugar or sweeteners or is fried. It's the food that can last on a kitchen bench for weeks and weeks before going mouldy: store-bought cookies, ice-cream, fries, chips, etc. These foods should definitely be eaten after real foods and in amounts that are minimal. Teach children that these foods will not add any nourishment to their bodies.

By classing food into groups and saying 'We eat real food first before we have processed food', we are guiding and teaching our children in a way they can understand. This is about teaching or coaching children about food. They need reasons why they cannot have ice-cream all day or chips for all snacks.

If your children ever ask about the food groups and why ice-cream is not a real food or why they need to eat real food before processed food, you can give a simple answer, such as 'Real food helps you to grow. It is alive food that offers your body nutrients and minerals [or "little helpers", depending on the children's age and level of comprehension], while processed food does not add to your body. It is okay to eat once in a while, but real food makes you __________ [fill in the blank for your child's specific interest, e.g. run fast, grow tall, have more energy].'

Find out what works for you. Although I started with using three levels, I now only use two. I say real food or alive food, and processed food. I put the emphasis on these foods and the rest — bread, etc — falls in-between depending on what they have been eating. I appreciate I am being vague, but remember often children do not need to box everything like we do. I found that using three levels was too hard a concept for my little ones to comprehend. However, my children could grasp that they had to have alive food, the food that would add to their bodies, before they had the food that would not give their bodies any of the good stuff.

(I refer to 'good stuff' in our household as like little people who help keep bodies healthy. These little people come to help build their bodies to make them strong and their brains to help them learn. I have found if you get into character when explaining this to your kids they get a really good mental image of the 'good stuff' in food you are talking about.)

But remember do what feels good for you, if you feel the need to do all three categories, then please do so.

Real food disguised as processed food

Watch out for real food disguised as processed food. No, that is not a typo. Remember, we are teaching habits. When you make a homemade ice-cream with frozen banana and strawberries, your children don't know it is healthy. All they see is that they get ice-cream for a snack every day. When they are little, this is more crucial, as they don't have the reasoning ability that older children have. As they get older you can relax on this a little more, because they see that this ice-cream is made of real food, unlike the ice-cream you buy from the supermarket. Little children cannot comprehend this and they grow up thinking it is okay to eat ice-cream for every snack.

Food should be enjoyed. How you see mealtimes, how you see your body and food, and how you classify food all affect your children's love or hate of food. Get clear in your head about food and what it signifies for you. Then you can teach your children about food more actively.

PART II

Foundations

CHAPTER FIVE

WHAT I WISH I HAD KNOWN BEFORE I HAD CHILDREN

Food, nutrition, what you 'allow' and the food you shelter your kids from can be a minefield. If you are like me — and I think most parents are — when you become pregnant, all or most of your energy is focused on getting through pregnancy and preparing for labour, with a little bit left over to actually think about the newborn stage. I remember I was given a baby plate and cutlery as a present before I had Huxley (my first daughter), and although I was very grateful for it, I did think 'What do I need this for?' Little did I know that time flew by and before I knew it I was up to my ears in puréed food!

This chapter would be ideal as a part of a 'new parents' handbook, but no matter how old your children are, it is never too late. I went through this process late as well, but it was the best thing I did.

This chapter is all about thinking about your deal-breakers and the boundaries you want to create for your children. By getting straight in your own head the bigger picture and then the boundaries or deal-breakers you want to have as a family, the easier life around food becomes. (By the way, don't assume you will be on the same page as your partner or any other adults who have or will have a lot to do with your children when you are not there. You must discuss these deal-breakers as a parent unit or caregiving unit to have the greatest impact on your children.)

I am not a big fan of shopping for shopping's sake, simply because when I don't know what I want, I get overwhelmed with the choices and will constantly question if I am making the right decision. But when I want or need something, I love to shop, surveying my options at each shop for that one item (say boots) then deciding which ones I like best and going back to that shop to buy them. For me, it's like a complete circle: I am happy with the boots I have chosen so I don't need to carry on looking. When we don't take time to decide what boundaries we want to make for our children, or take time to think of the bigger picture with food, the circle is still open. We are looking at other parents for options of how to do things; we ask or are looking to our parents and in-laws to see what they did when we were children;

we can even look to the preschool teacher who doesn't have children of her own. With all these different opinions and ways to parent, we are left with an overwhelming sense of either 'What am I doing wrong?' or 'What can I do better?'. Either way, you are constantly on the look-out for those boots, never feeling quite confident that the boots you have are the right ones.

I found that because I sat down to think about the bigger picture and outlined the boundaries I thought were going to be necessary to achieve that bigger picture, then spent some time getting on the same page as Ben, three things happened. Firstly, I was less overwhelmed whenever food options came up. For example, if we were out and it had been a few hours since we had had something to eat and we went by an ice-cream shop, before identifying our boundaries Ben and I would go back and forwards on whether we should give Huxley ice-cream on an empty stomach. Now I have a definite — real food first — so I will be on the look-out for something like sushi, with the possibility of going back for ice-cream later.

Secondly, as Ben and I were on the same page, we were both parenting more consistently. Food became less emotional as there was no 'Don't tell your mother I gave you this'. Thirdly, my confidence grew, which meant when someone did something differently or offered 'advice' about food and what 'I should do' I could easily decide if it was going to suit me or not. All in all, I was much less overwhelmed with what I was 'supposed' to do as I had already planned it!

I am excited about sharing this chapter with you as this is where you get to shine as a parent, where your confidence grows and your parenting around food is taken to the next level. After reading this chapter and sitting down with the Action Steps along the way, your parenting style will take a leap towards the coaching style. Why? Because you can create the boundaries that suit you and your family. You will have thought through the habits you want for your children and these habits will become a priority. But best of all, it puts you in the driving seat of teaching your children about food.

THE BIGGER PICTURE

Have you ever tried to look for something and not been able to find it, yet when you asked someone else they pointed out that it was right in front of you? When we get too narrow focused, we lose sight of what we are trying to achieve. Creating a healthy relationship with food in your children is no different. We get wrapped up in the day-to-day rather than seeing the bigger picture.

What do you want to achieve? What sort of children do you want to raise? Are you raising children to conform to everything you say? Or do you want to raise children who feel empowered, assert autonomy and have a healthy relationship with food?

When I learnt to do a layup in basketball, I learnt it in steps. First I did the footwork without the ball. Left, right, left (jumping straight up on left). Then I did it with the ball, with a bounce on the first step, but no shooting. Then I practised shooting off the backboard. Then put it all together: ball, footwork and shot. From here it progressed to how to fake someone, how to do a turn and shoot — many different combinations depending on what the defence was doing. I was given steps and guidelines to master before going on to the next step. The end result was always to get the ball in the hoop, as the goal was to win the game.

Feeding children is very similar. You need to define the goal or priority. It may be to foster a healthy relationship with food in your children, or it may be more happy children in general. You need to think how you will get to the goal.

In basketball, the goal is getting as many points as possible. In feeding children it is to develop healthy habits around food. The layup broken down into steps was just one way to reach that goal. Feeding children is much the same. We have a goal and there is a list of potential ways we can go about achieving that goal. Have you ever sat down to think about it? When you do, the steps — individual mealtimes — become clearer. Instilling a healthy relationship with food through forming healthy habits will be at the forefront of your mind, not the mindset of 'you must eat this lettuce'. It changes the way you interact with food and your children. Your parenting becomes more consistent and in line with the values you are trying to instil in your children.

When I was pregnant and I was asked whether I wanted a boy or a girl, I mostly gave the stock standard, politically correct answer: 'I don't care, as long as the baby is healthy.' I am sure you have also uttered these words. But we tend to get busy and so involved in life that we forget that we also want not only a healthy baby but also a healthy child, healthy teen and healthy adult.

Instilling healthy habits by providing guidelines for your children is the *how* — the getting shots in the goal. It will help you reach your overall goal of having healthy babies, children, teens and adults.

ACTION STEPS

1. What is the bigger picture that you would like for your children and food?
2. How do you think you can raise your children with the bigger picture in mind, e.g. if you have 'having a healthy relationship with food' as the bigger picture, what will get you there? Forcing broccoli down their throats or making healthy food fun?

DEAL-BREAKERS

What are deal-breakers? They are the things you think your children 'must do'. All parents have deal-breakers, yet sometimes they vary depending on what mood you are in.

Some deal-breakers exist to keep your children safe, like holding hands crossing the road. Other deal-breakers are not so much about keeping them safe but rather about your priorities as a parent, such as brushing their teeth before bed. Brushing their teeth every night is not going to keep your children safe (well, maybe from the drill of the dentist, but it's not a matter of life and death), it is a habit you enforce because you know it is good for them. So deal-breakers are habits you enforce because they make life safer for your children or you are looking after them in some way.

Your deal-breakers

This is when you get to define your deal-breakers around food. Later on in the chapter I will go through some food habits you may want to create, but the beauty with deal-breakers is that you get to define them with your own situation, priorities and lifestyle in mind.

Everybody will be different, and that is okay. I remember when Huxley was about 16 months and she went through a stage where she would throw an absolute tantrum when we tried to put shoes on her. Even if we got them on her without a fuss, she would often stop and take them off when we were out. While having no shoes on when walking down the street is commonplace and often acceptable in New Zealand, where Ben and I had grown up, England, walking around with bare feet is a social faux pas. Ben and I were constantly faced with a decision: do we force her to wear shoes with the probability of a complete meltdown and ruin her (and our) outing, or do we let it slide (not make it a deal-breaker)? We would often let it slide, choosing to use our energy to keep an eye out for glass rather than to enforce putting shoes on. One day a friend who had grown up in a wealthy nearby town was with us, and could not comprehend why we were okay with letting Huxley walk without shoes. Although he didn't have any children, wearing shoes would have been a deal-breaker for him. Nobody was right or wrong, we just had different priorities.

You and your partner

When defining the habits you want to create, it is important to be on the same page as your partner. If you have one agenda and your partner has another, it is very confusing for your children. You may need to soften your expectations a little, or you may need to indulge your partner a little on things that are important to them. Either way, you need to be on the same page.

Secondly, you need to think about what creating these habits means. It is easy to say that you would enforce always putting shoes on, yet when you are faced with a convulsing toddler, it may not seem like so much of an issue.

Keep in mind that you can change what you enforce in the future. Define what habits you want to create and after a week, month or year, if you are finding it is too much effort to create that habit, then it is okay to redefine it. As children grow older you will find that priorities change. Although holding your two-year-old's hand when you cross the road may be a deal-breaker, doing it when they're 16 is not. Things change.

Everybody is different. We have different priorities and different agendas. Create boundaries that fit into your lifestyle while thinking about the habits your children will learn from these boundaries.

CREATING HABITS

When well-meaning waiting staff would quietly ask if they could give my children lollies at the end of a meal, I always declined. The common response was, 'One won't hurt them. They have been so good', often accompanied with a look of disgust that I was depriving my children. I was well aware that one lolly would not hurt them, but that was not my reason for saying no. My reason centred on habits. At the forefront of my mind I had the thought 'What habit is this creating?' I didn't want my children to associate going out to dinner with getting lollies, and I didn't want to reward their good behaviour with sweets.

It is time to start to think about the habits you want to create. With the bigger, long-term picture in mind, start to think about what habits around food will help you achieve this. Here are a few things to ponder:

- Do you want any or all meals to be eaten with the whole family together (from daily meals such as dinner, to weekly meals like breakfast on Sundays)?
- Do you want your children to sit down every time they are eating, or just for meals?
- Do you want to have specific mealtimes or 'time zones', or are you happy with making and eating food when your kids become hungry? (Dina Rose in her book *It's Not About the Broccoli* says to set time or nutritional zones to help kids know when food will be served. Although I know this has helped many parents and could help you, especially if your kids are filling up on snacks before meals, having too much structure in my day overwhelms me — which then doesn't work well for my children.)
- Do you want to serve dessert every night?
- Are you happy with your children getting something to eat after dinner (or dessert), or is that the last meal of the day?
- What foods are you okay with having in the house — from ice-blocks to candy to chips to juice. If it is in your home, it will be become a 'normal' food for your children to have.
- Do you want to be more strict on food when your children are sick or if an illness is 'going around' your family or school? (Around 70–80 per cent of your body's immune cells are found in your gut,[16] therefore I think it makes sense that when you and your children are ill, or when there is a bug 'going around', your family shouldn't eat foods that are known to decrease immunity. If you are going to implement this, remember to talk to your kids about it so they can understand the reasoning behind it and it is not 'just because'.)

- If you have babies, do you want to restrict certain foods in their first one or two years of life, while their gut lining is developing? It makes sense in my mind to restrict or withhold foods that could comprise immunity during this period.

Keep pondering what habits you want to instil and what that entails. You can also think about the habits you wish you didn't have or did have surrounding food, or even the habits you love having.

Being realistic

Once you have decided on a few ideals and habits you want to instil, it is time to get realistic. This is where we think forward into our imaginary future and see if these habits will become our deal-breakers.

It was easy for me to think, 'Oh, when Huxley goes out she will always have shoes on when walking down the street', but like I said, when faced with a tantrum-throwing toddler, I chose not to enforce this habit. If it was a deal-breaker for me, I would have been stronger, knowing that once you create an expectation in your children, although it may end in tears the first few times, they will end up getting it.

So plan ahead. What ideals do you have for your children? If say, like myself, you decide to limit sugar in your children's diet before the age of two, you need to know you will be facing a few tricky situations. What happens when they go to a birthday party and all the other kids are getting cake and lollies? What happens when you are giving your older children some food with sugar in it — will the younger one miss out?

Once we prepare for what it means in our daily lives to instil this habit, we can work out how to execute it — say, in the example above, having no sugars unless given by others on the odd occasion like a birthday party, or when the cake comes out, you take your child away and play with them somewhere so they don't know what they are missing out on.

Reading the above, you may have had an emotional reaction. How can you take a kid away from cake, or even thinking about it in your personal situation: 'I could never have not given my kids sugar until age two.' Everybody is different; we all have different priorities and different views. If you really want something to happen, you will put the effort in and make it happen.

Also, keep in mind that the idea of creating habits is not to get children eating zero unhealthy food; it is fostering an idea that they can have anything they want to eat — they may even have lollies and biscuits — but instead of finishing the whole packet they will only take one or two. They will choose healthy food most of the time, because healthy food makes them feel good. They will have no emotional attachment to food.

ACTION STEPS

1. Sit down with you partner and list what food habits you want to create in your children (keeping the bigger picture in mind).
2. Look at your list, and for each habit write down some potential future situations where instilling these habits will become hard or nearly impossible to do.
3. What action plans (to keep with the habits you want to instil) can you put in place for these potential future situations?

Key habits

Now that you have decided on your key habits, I want to share mine with you. I have asked many adults, 'What habits do you wish you had around food?', as well as, 'What habits do you like having around food?' Children grow into adults, so asking adults what habits they want to have and then working backwards with ideas to instil these habits is a no-brainer.

Through all my questioning I have found some habits that kept popping up. These are the key habits that adults identified with having a healthy relationship with food:

1. hunger habits — checking-in and pausing
2. adventurous eaters (taste buds in training)
3. eating a variety of food
4. healthy snacking
5. starting the day right
6. not eating after dinner
7. pleasure from eating.

To reiterate, I am not saying that you should have all of these habits if you want to encourage a healthy relationship with food in your children, they are just the top habits adults wished they had. All of these are explored further in the upcoming chapters.

From my point of view, the first two are the foundations in encouraging children to have a healthy relationship with food. These two habits help children to create autonomy with food and to trust themselves. Both of the first two in the list above are large topics, so I have created a chapter for each of them (see chapters six and seven).

The others in the list are also priorities for me, so I will go through them briefly in chapter eight. But for now, I want to address a question I get a lot of the time — what about grandparents and other people who give your children food?

WHAT ABOUT OTHER PEOPLE?

Grandparents and other caregivers

I can feel the tension already. I would say about 90 per cent of parents have some sort of beef (excuse the pun) with either their parents or their in-laws or both when it comes to food and their children. On the flip side, I know that some (maybe most) grandparents or other significant caregivers also have a beef with you!

Grandparents have done it before. They raised you and maybe a few other children, and you turned out fine, so should we parent the way they did?

Absolutely not.

For a couple of reasons. To start with, food has changed. What my mother was having as a 'treat' growing up is common everyday food now and 'treats' have morphed and become Frankenfoods! Next, if we look at our health as a society — the rising obesity rate, chronic disease rates, etc — something is going haywire. I am not saying that what we do as this generation of parents will be the perfect answer, but to do what has been done before is clearly not working.

I am guessing most of you know this, which is why you are reading this book. But getting the grandparents on board can be a whole other issue! Although I don't have this perfect in my own life, there are a number of things you can do to help get the grandparents on board with what you do when it comes to food and your children.

Firstly, if you are confident in your deal-breakers and boundaries it is easier to talk to the grandparents about them, telling them the reasons why they are important to you and your priorities in raising your children. Most of the time, if you set out clear boundaries of what you expect them to provide or not provide to your children, with the reasons why, they will respect that.

Sometimes, however, they won't respect you and your choices, thinking they know best, or even feeling it is their right to have a say in their grandchildren's upbringing. Truth is, I am not too sure how I will react to my children and their partners doing something I don't agree with to my grandchildren! I won't know until I am a grandparent myself, but I do appreciate that it may be particularly hard for them, going from having complete control over raising their own children to taking a step back in helping to raise their grandchildren, whom they love so dearly. It takes a special sort of person to do something like not give a child lollies when they wholeheartedly believe it will do no harm — especially when food has been a way to show love in their experience. Go easy on them. Give them this book to read, have a heart-to-heart with them about your hopes and dreams, and show them the bigger picture, your bigger picture.

If that fails, I think you have two options. Firstly, ask yourself if it is time to lower your standards a little bit. If the answer is no, and it is a major source of contention between you and them, then what is the priority? Having grandparents in your children's lives who give them love and attention, albeit with lollies sometimes, *or* your children having a clean diet but less contact with their family? Again, everyone will have different grandparents to contend with as well as different priorities with food. It is not useful to you or your children for you to get worked up every time they stay at their grandparents' place because the grandparents don't parent exactly how you think they should. What are your priorities?

Judgement from others

Being a nutritionist, health and eating have always been priorities for me. I created boundaries that I thought would be good for my children early on. One of these boundaries was no added sugar before the age of two. I thought it would be the best start I could give my children, but I didn't enter into it lightly; I knew it would have its challenges. It was a boundary that I discussed with Ben, and he was happy to have it, so we were on the same page. What I wasn't quite prepared for, though, were the judgements that family and friends made of this boundary. 'Don't be so ridiculous, you're depriving them.' 'You may be able to do it with one, but you won't do it with your second or third.' 'But they like it.'

At first I got quite upset that people would judge me as a parent for the choices I made. It was so easy to judge them as well, yet deep down I didn't expect anyone to make the same choices that I made. It was my priority, not theirs. However, I continued to feel upset at people's judgements, especially my family's.

Then Ben said something that changed the way I viewed these judgements. He said, 'You know they are only judging you because they are not confident in their choices, and by doing things a different way it challenges them to reflect on themselves.' While this may not always be the case, I have found it to be true in so many circumstances. If I met these judgements with justification and tried to prove why my way was better, people got defensive. They shut down and wanted to prove the opposite was better, their way. Their minds closed off to the possibility that there was another way that they had not or had yet to consider.

When you meet these types of judgements without trying to justify your case, even the most hardened of people may actually see your point of view. If not, it doesn't really matter. By respecting their decision they are more likely to respect yours, rather than judge you.

Well done! If you have sat down and reflected on the bigger picture, thought about habits, what creating those habits will mean and also how you are going to bring the grandparents or other caregivers on board, you are well on your way to creating a healthy relationship with food in your children. If you have not done this already, stop reading, get a pen and paper, call a meeting (or a chin-wag as Ben and I call it) with your partner and get thinking.

From here on in we get practical — taking the journey from how to create these habits to getting your children involved and even taking it a step further and going through what I call 'foodication', my system for creating 'foodies' or adventurous eaters out of your children.

CHAPTER SIX

HUNGER HABITS

Imagine if everyone relied on internal cues to start and stop eating, rather than external cues. I have asked many people what food habits they wished they had. Only eating when hungry and not stuffing themselves until they are uncomfortably full is one habit that most people wished they had. 'Checking-in', as discussed in this chapter, is a habit that will help with this, and it also has a greater potential. If you believe that one man's diet is another man's poison, then developing the habit of checking-in will help children to grow up with a sense of what foods add to their energy and what foods take away. They won't have to be told what to eat by the government or Jenny Craig — they will grow up with a sense of what foods make *them* feel healthy. That is a healthy relationship with food in full action!

Parents have a unique opportunity to teach children how to follow internal versus external hunger cues. Habits are subconscious and automatic, we don't think about them. Creating a habit of checking-in before and during eating can only help children develop a healthy relationship with food and will give them the power to decide whether they are hungry and how much they want to eat. Teaching children to check-in may be tedious at first, but when it becomes their subconscious habit — whoa, imagine the results!

Advertising and food companies are always studying how they can get people to buy their food, from serving sizes to bright labels to developing a perception that you are cool if you drink or eat their product. There are also a lot of lobbyists trying to limit how companies advertise their products. While I agree there should be limitations on advertising, we as parents can still teach our children to have individual thought over their behavioural choices.

I was at a playground a few years ago and a three-year-old was climbing up the 'big kids' ladder. Rasmus was climbing close behind. As I was keeping an eye on my youngest, Eckhart, I heard the dreaded scream. Was that my child? As I looked around, the boy in front had fallen on Rasmus and knocked him off the ladder. Both were on the ground crying. As I picked up Rasmus to give him a cuddle, the mother of the boy who had knocked him off was frantic. 'Oh, I am so sorry. I never let him climb this. It was his first time. I am so sorry! Is your son okay?' Rasmus was fine, just a little startled. Two minutes of cuddles and he was off playing again. The mother continued to apologise and say that she wouldn't be letting her son go up there again. I watched as for the next half-hour she either took her son away from the ladder or carried him up it.

My thought process was a little different. How did she expect her son to learn how to climb a ladder if she never let him? Of course he will fall down when he first tries; that is all a part of learning. Gradually he will get better and better.

Food is the same. You can either not let your children try, or be right behind them when they show interest in trying and, when they do fall, be there to catch them until they build up the coordination to take on the task all by themselves. You can guide your children to seek food that makes them feel awesome. This is a learnt skill, something that they will gradually get better at.

Food companies are always going to be there trying to influence children to eat what they have made — healthy or not. It's a given. Parents can help to decrease their influence by throwing out the TV (which I highly recommend, though I know it's not for everyone), but we cannot eliminate advertising influence all together. It's going to affect them, if not as children it will as adults. Developing a habit of checking-in will help to decrease the influence advertising has on your children, and encourage them to follow internal cues rather than external ones.

Checking-in periodically will develop a habit: children who will eat independent of situations, and later adults who will eat when they feel hungry, who choose food that feels good for them, and who will stop eating before they feel stuffed. This will be as natural to them as it is for you to stop at a stop sign, or to brush your teeth before going to bed.

CHECKING-IN

Developing the habit of checking-in before, during and after meals is pretty simple, really. It involves creating a conversation around how your children feel and getting them to make connections between the sensations they have in their bodies and the food they eat.

Before they start eating

When children say they are hungry, ask them where they feel it, and what the sensation feels like. If it had a colour, what would it be? If it had a texture, what would it be? Ask them to describe it in as much detail as possible.

The age of your children and the situation you are in will reflect how much questioning you do and the tone of your questioning. I know if I came home from a long day, having not eaten much, and Ben started to ask me about where I was feeling the hunger and to describe the sensation, I would probably be a bit annoyed. You don't need to do it all the time; choose times to be inquisitive with your children. Or perhaps, if they are older, you can tell them you are reading a book about how they can develop a healthy relationship with food and how you wish you had known this growing up. Speaking to your children openly and honestly about what you wish for them and how it will help them now and in the long run will develop a deeper relationship with them.

If they are too young to participate, then speak about yourself. 'Mummy is hungry. I can tell I am hungry because I can feel an emptiness in my stomach. It feels like an empty green room.' Or even, 'I am not that hungry at the moment, but I feel that a crisp apple may give me more energy to play with you.' After eating, you could say if it helped or didn't help to energise you. The point is not to be right, but to create an awareness of why you choose to eat — without judgement.

While eating

Serving food on a big plate, in a big bag or in any sort of big package influences people to eat more. Having food in sight, either on the table or laid out buffet-style also influences people to eat more.[17] We tend to eat with our eyes more than our stomach. Awareness around eating helps to decrease this influence on us.

Develop a conversation around food with your children while you are eating. How does food feel, the texture, temperature? What do you like about it? What don't you like about it? How does it feel in your body? Talk about savouring the food. Does it give your body energy? Talking about their experiences will help them make connections with how they see and feel towards food. Again, the age of your children will influence how much detail you go into.

In Brian Wansink's book *Mindless Eating,* he identifies three levels of fullness:

1. starving
2. could eat more
3. stuffed.

While eating, if your attention is directed towards how the food makes you feel, you are more likely to stop eating before you feel over-full. Talk to your kids about how you stop eating when you no longer feel hungry, rather than when you feel full. Or even use the word *satisfied.* You can be full and not satisfied, or satisfied and not full. By emphasising satisfied, your children are less likely to develop a habit of eating to the point of feeling stuffed and are more likely to eat because of internal cues, like satisfying hunger.

Asking your children what hunger feels like and where they feel it will also re-emphasise being in tune with their bodies while eating. They will develop a habit of checking-in to see if what they are eating is 'sitting well' with them (not making them feel bloated or anxious, etc). When they say, 'I am not hungry anymore', ask them how they know. Sometimes they will say one-liners that suggest they are not interested in talking about it; other times the conversation will be more in-depth. The answers don't matter, it is the message that counts: the message of constantly checking-in, to see how food feels for them.

It can feel tedious as a parent to ask all these questions, but the consequences are worth it. One day Ben took Huxley to a movie and she asked for something to eat. 'Can I have ice-cream? Oh, and popcorn. How about some . . .' Ben said she could have a choice of one thing. She chose the ice-cream. She was really proud when she came home and told me how she got half-way through the ice-cream and started to feel yucky inside, so she threw it away. In her words, 'I enjoyed the first bit, but it was too much for me to eat.' Although this is still an ongoing journey for our family, in this moment I could see that my efforts to get her to check-in were paying off. Yours will, too.

After eating

Developing a habit of checking-in after meals includes thinking about how the food makes you feel *after* you have finished eating. I have used this question with all of my children, and I had a proud-mum moment a few months ago when my daughter turned down some marshmallows. When her grandmother asked why, she said, 'I don't feel that well and they will just make me feel worse.' She had never told me before that marshmallows made her feel not that well, maybe because she thought I would never let her have them again! But she did have the ability to turn them down when she wasn't feeling 100 per cent.

Checking-in after meals creates responsibility in your children: the ability to actively think about how food affects them. They will respond accordingly, eventually. They just need room to experience and practise it first.

Develop checking-in before, during and after meals. Children will become more in tune with their bodies. They will go through experiences where they will choose unhealthy food; perhaps they will even binge on it. But if they are constantly checking-in they will come to realise that these foods do not make them feel good. They will grow up with the ability to choose foods that feel good for them, not because they 'should' but because this food satisfies them and makes them feel energised.

PAUSING

Often what we decide to eat or carry on eating is not because of hunger but because of other emotional and psychological reasons. When I asked adults what habits they wished they had around food, an overwhelming number of people ranked wanting to eat because they truly wanted to, not because they were influenced by their emotions or surroundings. While checking-in will help to instil this relationship with food, it is still not enough.

Variations on 'Once you start you just cannot stop' are a slogan in much food advertising. I have experienced this many times. Wrapped up on the couch with the wind howling outside, either reading a book or watching a movie, feeling like a bit of comfort, I open a packet of biscuits. Half an hour later and I am looking at Ben in disgust: he ate all the damn biscuits! How dare he! He registers my disgust and looks down. 'Where did all the biscuits go? I only got one,' he says. Reality kicks in. I have just polished off a full packet of biscuits, but worst of all I had not even realised it. I am sure Ben had a few more than one . . .

Distracted eating is disastrous. You eat more than you need and you don't even remember! If you think this doesn't happen to you, don't count on it — so did many of the participants in a study done by Brian Wansink. He found that most people eating when distracted (e.g. watching a movie) will eat more but remember less. Just because you don't remember doesn't mean it didn't happen!

I have also tried to be 'good'. I thought taking a few biscuits and leaving the packet in the pantry would decrease the amount I ate. That way I would know what I had eaten. However, I would still get up from my cosy couch and raid the pantry for a few more biscuits about four times before I thought I had had enough. I would eat only half the packet, but I would do it without thinking. I would feel deprived that I could only have a couple of biscuits, and that would set my cravings into overdrive. I want more, I need more.

I am sure I don't need to tell you that deprivation diets don't work. The more you say no to something, the more your brain cannot let go of it and the more it makes you want it. The cravings intensify.

The key to overcoming these types of unhealthy obsession with food and to eliminating overeating is to create a habit of a pause. Pause before all meals, snacks and drinks.

Creating the habit of a pause brings your awareness back to eating itself. Essentially you are being mindful about eating. Before you think I am being all 'woo-woo' about eating, I am not advocating 'mindful eating'. Although I think it is a great practice to have, realistically, locking yourself away and eating with your full attention on your food is not practical. But practising mindfulness in periods while eating is doable.

This may take some practice as an adult, as it can seem overwhelming. But imagine if this habit was instilled into children from day one: that pausing before having food and while having food was just something they did. Initially, it will be something you teach them, but as they grow older it will be something they just do, a subconscious habit. What a great habit to have!

I get excited when I think about a generation growing up with the ability to pause before and during meals — not because they will not ever eat unhealthy food, but because they will have conscious control and autonomy over what they are eating. If they are eating only because they smelt the food and it smells good, they will know. They will eat responsibly, have the ability to respond to eating cues, and not be subconsciously affected by external food cues.

Creating a habit of pausing creates an awareness of what they are about to eat. Creating this awareness can influence what and how much they will eat, if not in that moment but the next time they are offered the same food. Children will develop a habit of subconsciously choosing food that is good for them and will be less influenced by external cues.

Pause before

There are a number of ways to help create a pause. The goal is not for your children to not want to eat; the goal is to create a pause so they become aware of their eating.

Saying grace is a pause that some religions adopt. If your family has a habit of saying grace before dinner, but you close your eyes, make it a habit to consciously eye the food after grace has been said. Even add a statement like, 'Look at this wonderful food we have', even if it is just beans on toast. Children may not seem like they are listening, but they are. This will become a habit.

If you are not religious and saying grace feels weird for you, then give 'making speeches' a go. This has the added benefit of giving children confidence in public speaking. Ben brought this into our home. Every meal we sit down to, Ben or I will say, 'Who is giving a toast tonight?' Sometimes all of the children will say something. If they don't feel like it, Ben or I will do the honours. Ben normally leads the way and gives structure to his own toast by thanking the cook or even the farmers who grew the food, thereby drawing attention to the food about to be eaten; saying what he enjoyed about the day; sometimes pointing out something that the children have done which he thought was awesome. Our children follow this lead, and when they give a toast it is natural for them to thank the cook, often while eyeing the food, welcome guests if we have them, and say something they enjoyed about the day. A great pause to start the meal.

You can also create a pause by asking questions. My favourite is asking my children whose favourite food they think this might be or, as Brian Wansink suggests, asking, 'Would Batman [or one of their heroes] eat this?' It doesn't matter what they answer; the point is that they have created a pause and eyed the food they are about to eat. This creates an awareness of what they are about to eat. Creating this awareness can influence what and how much they will eat, if not in that moment then the next time they are offered the same food. Children will develop a habit of subconsciously choosing food that is good for them.

Creating a pause before a meal or snack also gives you the opportunity to add in a descriptive name for the meal. If you are serving your children a new food item you are unsure whether they will like, then giving it a cool descriptive name will help them develop positive associations towards that item. For example, 'Thanks, Ben, for cooking. The dinosaur trees gently sautéed in butter smell amazing.' (See page 154 for more descriptive names.) Creating a positive expectation will not guarantee that your children will finish all of their broccoli, but you have a better chance.

When your children ask for a certain food, ask them why they feel like eating it. Whether or not you will give it to them, it will create a pause. They may not be able to answer you all the time, but getting their brains ticking over about why they want to eat that food will create an awareness of why they choose certain food. Even if it's 'it smells good' or 'it looks cool', they are teaching themselves that they are eating for other reasons than practical hunger. They may still be influenced by external cues, but they will be aware that they are being influenced. They will become more aware when they are being affected by emotions and you can then teach them there are ways to satisfy those emotions other than with food. Instead of growing up with guilt attached to food, they will grow up with awareness of food.

Pause during

Creating a pause during meals is a bit more difficult. However, it is still possible. It will be you they are learning from. Just like I learnt to eat fast from my mum, your children can learn to eat slowly from you. By eating slowly and putting your fork down between bites, you will show your children that this is the way you eat.

When I went to university, Sunday lunches were a formal occasion. The students all came in and sat down and got served as you would at a restaurant (everyone took their turns at being the server). The dishes were not cleared until everyone had finished eating.

Another student, who I became close friends with, was the slowest eater in the room. (I was the fastest.) I could not understand why he took so long to eat. A few years passed and I went to dinner with him and his brother. I had to laugh when I realised that his brother ate even more slowly than he did! Slow was what they knew; their parents were slow eaters, they were slow eaters, it was not a conscious decision but a learnt one.

Develop yourself a habit of pausing between bites. Put your fork down, chat, make dinner time an experience to connect with your children, not just an eating experience. This will also help to make dinner times happier. Research suggests that happy people choose better food.

You can also ask your children where they feel the food if you think they are eating too much. Ask them how they know they are still hungry. This creates a pause and they are better able to comprehend when they are no longer hungry, when they are satisfied. (See also Tastication in chapter ten, where you will get a sense of what questions to ask to draw their attention to their taste buds.)

Pause at the end of the meal

Do something to signal the end of the meal. When we grew up it was drummed into us to put our knife and fork to the side to indicate we were finished. It was good manners.

Although this was taught by my parents as a polite way to say to the host that you are finished, it has inadvertently become a way to signal to myself that I have finished. A pause. Even to this day, putting my knife and fork to the side is a signal that I have finished, more so for myself than as a politeness towards others. Very rarely will I eat more after I have put my knife and fork to the side. This pause gives me the ability to consciously think about whether I want seconds or if I am satisfied.

If you don't like the idea of putting your knife and fork to the side, then develop a signal that identifies that you are finished with your meal. It could be a touch of the belly and a phrase: 'Yep, I am satisfied.' Teach this to your children.

Developing a pause before eating creates an awareness of what is about to be eaten. When done in conjunction with checking-in, it will instil a habit of relying on internal cues to eat. The environment in which your children eat will have less effect on them. Also, emotional attachment to food will decrease, and even when there is an emotional attachment your children will be conscious of it. They will be responsible with their emotions and food, and will have the ability to respond.

I am sure if everyone had this habit, obesity and health issues induced by a bad diet would decrease dramatically.

ACTION STEPS

1. Talk to your children about hunger levels and satisfaction levels. Ask them where they feel it physically. Ask them what their belly is telling them. Instead of saying 'Are you sure you're not hungry?', say 'How do you know your tummy is not hungry? What do you feel?'
2. Take the next best opportunity to talk about hunger in a way that your child will understand and will be meaningful to them. I have had clients do a drawing of five different bodies and a circle, with hungry being nothing in the circle, to over-full, where the whole circle is coloured in. I personally use a hand level: by the belly button is empty, at the neck is satisfied and to the eyes is over-full.

Note: Ensure you ask in an inquisitive tone, a tone that suggests 'I am interested in you and what you are feeling', and at a time when they are not so hungry that they get angry at you for not listening to them and asking silly questions!

CHAPTER SEVEN

TRAINING TASTE

You want to raise children who grow into adults who not only eat healthy food, but enjoy eating this healthy food. Coaching children, guiding children to try new food, to develop a taste for food, as well as creating healthy hunger habits, is the foundation.

Parents often think, either consciously or subconsciously like I did, that taste preferences are pre-established; that we offer children food until we find out what they like. When they turn their noses up at a food, we say 'oh no, she/he doesn't like that', thinking that their taste buds will mature later on.

This is not the case. We develop a taste for foods. Some children (and adults) take about 10–15 times of trying a new food to like it. It is not hate one day, like the next. It is a process, a journey. What we do to encourage this journey will affect our children.

For example, if we tell our children that they will like this food, they just need to try it first, some children may want to prove us wrong. They have made up their minds even before they try. This is where it is imperative to make this process a fun one.

I have developed a way to make this process fun, which will be covered in Foodication (chapter eleven), but for now let's look at some foundations.

FOUNDATIONS

I like to think of eating and learning to like foods such as vegetables as a process just like learning to ride a bike. The first time we try to ride a bike it is not all that fun. We are nervous and scared. We don't want to fall and hurt ourselves. And sometimes we do fall and get hurt. Yet this is an accepted part of learning to ride a bike. The more we practise, the more enjoyable an experience we have. Eating vegetables or healthy food is the same.

When we try a new food, the texture or taste can be different to what we have previously encountered. We can interpret this as unappealing and not fun. However, the more we try the food, the more we become accustomed to eating these foods and the more enjoyable the experience becomes.

If you think about 'training taste buds' when encouraging children to eat healthier foods, the tone and the message behind your words changes. It teaches children that healthy food is not only good for you but tastes amazing.

This is easy to say. When you have a defiant child sitting in front of you at dinner time it is hard not to use some of the methods we have discussed already — reward, punishment, etc. What follows next are ways to help your children to try new foods, from developing a positive eating atmosphere to what you can do directly to encourage them.

If you have children who are picky eaters or afraid of new foods, what follows next is especially important — for you and for them. Whether you like to admit it or not, you have a restricted view on food. I know I did — actually I still do, but I am learning to be more open. Before I had children I thought children either liked certain foods or they didn't. Children like sweets more than vegetables, and there was nothing parents could do about it.

While it is true that children have preferences towards certain foods (often foods that their mother ate while pregnant or when breastfeeding), this is not the end of the story. We can use this as an excuse, or we can accept what we cannot change and have the courage to change what we can. Taste buds are not set in stone. I used to hate olives. It wasn't so much about the taste, but the slimy texture. Gross. My friend Jamie sympathised with me and said, 'Yeah, I didn't like them either, but then I had three olives back to back and now I love them!' Dubious but intrigued, I gave it a go. One, gross. Two, still gross. Three, umm, less gross. It didn't really work, but something had changed in me that day. Although I didn't develop a liking for olives, I was more inclined to try them from that day onwards. When I was offered one as a snack, sometimes I would have one, other times none. But the more I saw them, the more I tried them. Although I still do not buy olives because I don't absolutely love them, I will eat them if they are there. I don't ask for the no-olive option when ordering a Greek salad. I gradually, over time, 'trained' my taste buds to like something I had previously thought was gross. I don't expect all children (or adults) to like all foods, but rather, instead of limiting our children (or ourselves) because we have made our minds up that we or they do not like a certain food, we can keep an open mind.

Thinking about children having taste buds 'in training' can help you and them to keep trying new foods. It can become a fun experiment rather than a 'you must eat this food!' experience. It can be an experience which they can feel empowered by. Forcing them to try food or developing a rigid control over their taste preferences often ends in them not wanting to like a food, just to prove you wrong. By allowing them the space to try food, they will feel empowered by their growing liking of new foods. It creates a sense of autonomy and shows them that you trust them to make good food choices, ultimately leading them to trust *themselves* with food.

Positive eating atmosphere — it starts with you

To grow the habit of training taste buds in your children, it is firstly important for *you* to grow this habit. If your children see you trying foods that you are unfamiliar with, you will lead by example. Who knows, you may even develop a liking for a food that you didn't think would be nice or had labelled as yuck long ago!

Also, it starts with your energy. If you have a negative association with your children trying new food, it will be a negative experience for them, and for you. Re-read chapter one if you need to go over how important you are as a role model in encouraging your children to eat more of the healthy stuff.

It is important for you to not expect children to like something the first time they try it. Realising that they may have to try it 15 different times, or prepared differently, helps.

Be honest and expect less

Practically, the first thing you can do is to be honest with your children. Teach them that they have taste buds in training.

You can do this in a variety of ways. I have found teaching them directly works well with young children, partly because they will believe anything you say. For older children, this often doesn't work. By age eight, children are starting to reason more and they want more than ever to assert their independence. To admit you are wrong once you have stated you don't like something is hard to do for adults, especially when someone is trying to persuade you otherwise. For children it is even harder.

As parents we can set up our children (inadvertently, of course) to dig their toes in and try to justify why they don't like a food. Even if they think the food starts to taste better the more they try it, they will never admit this to you. I have found indirectly teaching, by using made-up stories or relevant books (check out *Huxley the Duckling*),[18] or even asking them, for example, if they think garlic spinach is Popeye's favourite way of eating spinach, works best for older children. What is important is that you don't force your view onto your children, but provide a space where they can draw positive conclusions about the food first. They may not try it the first time but they will gradually be more open to trying different foods. The less you expect and the more you celebrate small wins, such as putting the tiniest of morsels in their mouths, the quicker your children will develop a trust in you and the more likely they will be to gradually try more different foods.

If your children take a bite of a new food and want to spit it out, let them do this. Firstly, yay! You got them to try a new food! Secondly, you can use this as an opportunity to teach them what adults do when they taste something they don't like. You can teach them that it is okay (if you think it is) to spit food out when you are with just your immediate family, but when you are out it is more polite to do what adults do, and show them how you take a sip of water to wash it down.

Teach them how to react and how to be polite. Remember, they don't know what they have not learnt.

Enlist other children

Another way to get your children to try new foods is to enlist other children. When children see other children eating something, especially if the children are older than yours, they will be more likely to try it. Dining with other children who you know eat a certain vegetable your child does not like can be a step towards getting your child to at least try this vegetable.

The opposite is also true. I am not a big fan of peas (although I am training myself to form a taste for them), I don't like them not because of their taste, but because my older sister didn't like them. I can clearly remember wanting to be like her and she didn't like peas.

Create a happy eating environment

Dinner times can be tense. You put effort into preparing meals with the expectation that your children will eat the healthy food you have prepared. I cannot speak for you, but I know I have taken offense at times when my efforts have been met with an 'Ew, this is yuck.' Or even if there is no vocalising, they refuse to eat what is on their plate. It can be a hit to the ego. Tension can mount and the dinner table becomes more like a war zone than a scene from *The Brady Bunch*.

This is when control can come into play. I know that on more than one occasion I have reverted to my five-year-old self and become so rigid in my expectations that I have met the children with tension rather than empathy. A friend of mine introduced me to Janet Lansbury's parenting blog (www.janetlansbury.com) and I instantly loved it. Whenever I read one of her articles about creating autonomy and meeting children with warmth I would always think about mealtimes. How is my tension influencing their healthy eating habits?

With tension, either from your own anxieties around food or your anxiety surrounding what your children 'should eat', you create a space for children to react defensively and negatively towards food. This ends badly. Children raised with adults who have anxiety around food are much more likely to experience less self-control and eat less fruit and vegetables[19] — the opposite of what I want. Janet Lansbury believes in justifying children's feelings, meeting them with warmth and creating a space for them to create autonomy, much like being a coaching parent.

After reading a few articles I decided to try this approach with my children. When the 'Ew, this is yuck' was said, I would reply, 'I can see you think you don't like it. I was like that when I was little. I would decide that food was yuck and I wouldn't try it. For years I didn't like avocado, because I thought it looked like green mash. But I am so glad I got the courage to try it, because now I love it.' I offered no words along the lines of 'You must eat it, or try it.' I simply justified their feelings and told them a story about myself. If they decided they were not hungry after one or two bites of a meal, I would just say, 'Okay, I'll leave it out for you to have if you get hungry later on.' If they got hungry later on, I would offer them their dinner again. Sometimes this would go smoothly, sometimes not so much. But I did notice that the energy of the eating environment changed. No longer was there a power struggle or tension. I provided the boundaries and the energy, and my children slowly began to follow suit. They could see they would get no reaction from me when they didn't want to try food or eat all their meal. Now the children will sometimes finish everything on their plate, even if it is mostly vegetables, and some days they won't eat much at all. When you trust your children, they end up trusting themselves.

MUSIC

Music is often played without people thinking about what effects it is having. Did you know that diners are more likely to eat faster and spend less time in a restaurant if there is upbeat music playing?[20] I laughed the first time I heard this, as I had a flashback to a time when I was in a noodle house and they were playing some crazy, upbeat music. I found myself stuffing in the food as fast as possible. I was about three-quarters of the way through my meal when I realised I was stressing out because I couldn't eat fast enough. As I paused, I realised I was eating in time to the music. It really confused me that the fast music could influence how I ate. This meant great turnover for that busy little noodle house, but it was terrible for my digestion!

Music has been shown to influence how much you eat, how fast you eat and how satisfied you are after the meal.[21] Playing some soft music at dinner time helps to create an environment that is relaxed and happy. If you don't believe me, try playing some heavy metal one evening and see how your children react, versus some soft, relaxing music another evening. My bet is that you won't be putting on that heavy metal music too often in the future!

Music can also get people dancing and in a relaxed mood. Try playing some of your favourite positive music when cooking dinner. Having the children dancing at your feet (away from hot pots, of course) while you cook dinner is a super-relaxing and happy way to start mealtime routines. Starting mealtimes like this may not guarantee a peaceful dinner time, but it will be more likely.

DISTRACTION

As mentioned above, distractions around mealtimes can be disastrous. I don't know about you, but I know that my concentration levels dramatically decrease when there is a lot going on.

Being distracted means you cannot give your children the attention they need. Also, when they are distracted they are more likely to eat faster, feel less full from a meal and not remember what they have eaten — not habits that are going to instil a healthy relationship with food.

Distractions are anything that takes away the attention from eating. Music can be a distraction, but if soft, calm music is a part of the background noise it can be beneficial. TV is a huge distraction for both you and the children. I remember getting told to 'sssshhh' when the news was on while we had dinner growing up. Conversation died and we all were glued to the TV.

What is more important, creating happy mealtimes for your children or watching something that you have forgotten about the next day? Keeping distractions to a minimum will help children to develop autonomy with their eating and will ultimately be a recipe for a pleasurable eating experience.

The environment you create around eating times covers many aspects, from the way you announce dinner ('Come to eat dinner, now!' versus 'Time to eat, guys!') to the way you set the table and the energy you bring to the table.

Create a happy eating environment for yourself, and your children will follow suit. Be present for your children and leave your day behind. Use it as a time to connect with your children over food and talk about the day. A good friend of mine uses this time for the family to share 'funnies and favourites', when their children are encouraged to share a story of their funniest moment and their favourite moment during the day. For some people, especially if you have teenagers, this may be the only time of the day you get to connect with your children.

ACTION STEPS

Make an effort tonight to keep the atmosphere at the dinner table positive, lower your expectations (or drop them), put on some soft, happy music, dance before dinner, and give your your full attention to your children. Bring a level of happiness within yourself to the dinner table and see how it affects your children.

ENCOURAGING TASTE BUDS IN TRAINING

Incorporating new foods into your children's diet can be daunting. They can kick up a fuss and fights can break out. This is one area which most parents struggle with. This section will make it easier on you.

However, do keep in mind that it is about habits. Your children will go through stages where they will not welcome new foods and will be very rigid about even looking at anything new. The most important thing you can do is keep these times positive or neutral. This gives them space to have their wobbly, but they will be more likely to try a food the next time around.

I learnt this the hard way when trying to get my children to eat salad. They had such negative associations with the word 'salad' that I still don't call a green salad just salad, I use some descriptive name, such as 'Popeye's favourite meal' (see page 154 for more details).

Keep all interactions positive or neutral. Some nights they will try the food, others they won't. What matters is that they will have a positive association with food that will lead to a healthy relationship with food.

Descriptive names

When I was cooking and serving something new, my husband often asked 'What do you call that?' I would always answer with the most unimaginative description. Garden salad with homemade dressing. Chicken wrapped in bacon. I have a hard time thinking of creative things on the spot, so would simply say what it was.

Have you ever been at a restaurant where they described the roast chicken and potatoes as 'Golden Roasted Chicken Served with Crisp Seasoned Roasted Vegetables' or the fish and chips as 'Succulent Fresh Fish with Home-style Just-dug Potatoes'? I think you can make up your own mind which meal sounds more appealing.

Children and adults are influenced by words. Research has shown that the name given to foods can influence not only what people ordered but how they rated the food.[22] Researchers took six different foods and put it on a university cafeteria menu. Each week for six weeks, two items were written down with the same basic, boring name, two with descriptive names and two were left off the menu. This process was repeated over six weeks, with all of the foods having a turn at being described with a boring name, a descriptive name or being left off the menu. 'Seafood Fillet' was labelled 'Succulent Italian Seafood Fillet', and 'Red Beans with Rice' was called 'Traditional Cajun Red Beans with Rice'. When the food was labelled with the descriptive name, 27 per cent more of it was ordered than when it was given just a normal name. Not only that, but eaters rated the items given descriptive names as being more appealing and tastier. They were identical foods, just named differently!

Descriptive menus, however, have been shown to not only increase the diner's expectation, which will in turn influence the experience, but also increase satiety after eating the meal.[23]

If you are serving a food to children and you use the word succulent, it will more than likely go over their heads. So attaching names that they can relate to would be much more appealing. Turn 'salmon with broccoli' into 'Salmon good enough for eagles, with dinosaur trees'.

See the next page for more ideas about how to create descriptive names for your children. Set a positive expectation for how vegetables or another healthy food will taste and you will more likely get a positive response to it.

I have personally found giving food descriptive names very successful. Once I was at my mother's for dinner. She was serving pumpkin. I had not cooked pumpkin that much at that time and so, although it was not a new food, the children had not had it in a long time. I thought it might become something left on the plate, with the children too afraid to try it. When I eyed my food I said, 'Oh, what a delicious sunshine-yellow pumpkin.' Rasmus didn't need any more encouragement and because Rasmus ate his pumpkin, his sisters followed!

Below is a list of descriptive name suggestions. You can name food anything you like. Is Dr Seuss not enjoyable because he made up many names and words in his stories?

Write down the descriptive names as a dinner menu. If your children are just learning to read they will take pride in 'announcing' what is for dinner. Or if they cannot read they will be intrigued by what it says.

DESCRIPTIVE NAME IDEAS			
HAPPY ASSOCIATION	PICKED AND PREPARED	SENSORY	LABEL/ STORY
Nana's	farm-fresh	succulent	dinosaur trees
summertime	just-dug	sunshine yellow	Popeye's favourite
lovingly prepared	freshly cut	juicy	Arctic trees
sunkissed	slow-cooked	crisp	the best
name of holiday spot	gently sautéed	seasoned	fresh
fun-loving	vine-ready	warming	the weirdest
	smashed-up	coolest	the oddest
		creamy	[your pet's] favourite
		divine	fit for a prince/ princess
			dragon-flame cooked

Make new food not new

Children have a tendency to reject new food — it is a natural part of growing up. So don't make new food new! Put it on the table, without putting it on their plate, for them to eye it. Develop a conversation about the food, making up a story about when you first tried it, or even a 'make-believe' story about it if you like making up stories. Create a positive association towards the food, like giving it a descriptive name. Don't even ask them to try it, just get them to see and talk about it.

You can also make it fun to 'try new things' by picking a 'weird' vegetable or fruit that they want to grow, or even make a game out of picking the weirdest fruit or vegetable from the supermarket and preparing it in a way that tastes good.

It is important not to be judgemental of your children if they decide they don't like a new food. Use it as a chance to not give up and instead say something like 'Great! We have found a way you don't like to eat it, so we can cross that one off the list. What other ways do you think we can cook/prepare it that may make it taste better?'

The more positive associations that you make with the food, either through a positive expectation of the taste or experience cooking or growing it, the higher the chances that your children will learn to try a new food and also continue to try it.

The following steps will help to make new food not new. Just by putting the new food on the table for your children to see, without expecting them to try it, describing it and telling stories about it, will set them up to be more intuitive.

The full technique is a seven-step process, but it can take just two. Just go with it. Sometimes they may still be unwilling to try it after the sixth step. In that case, leave it off the menu for a little bit then go back to step five, making different positive associations.

MAKING NEW FOOD NOT NEW

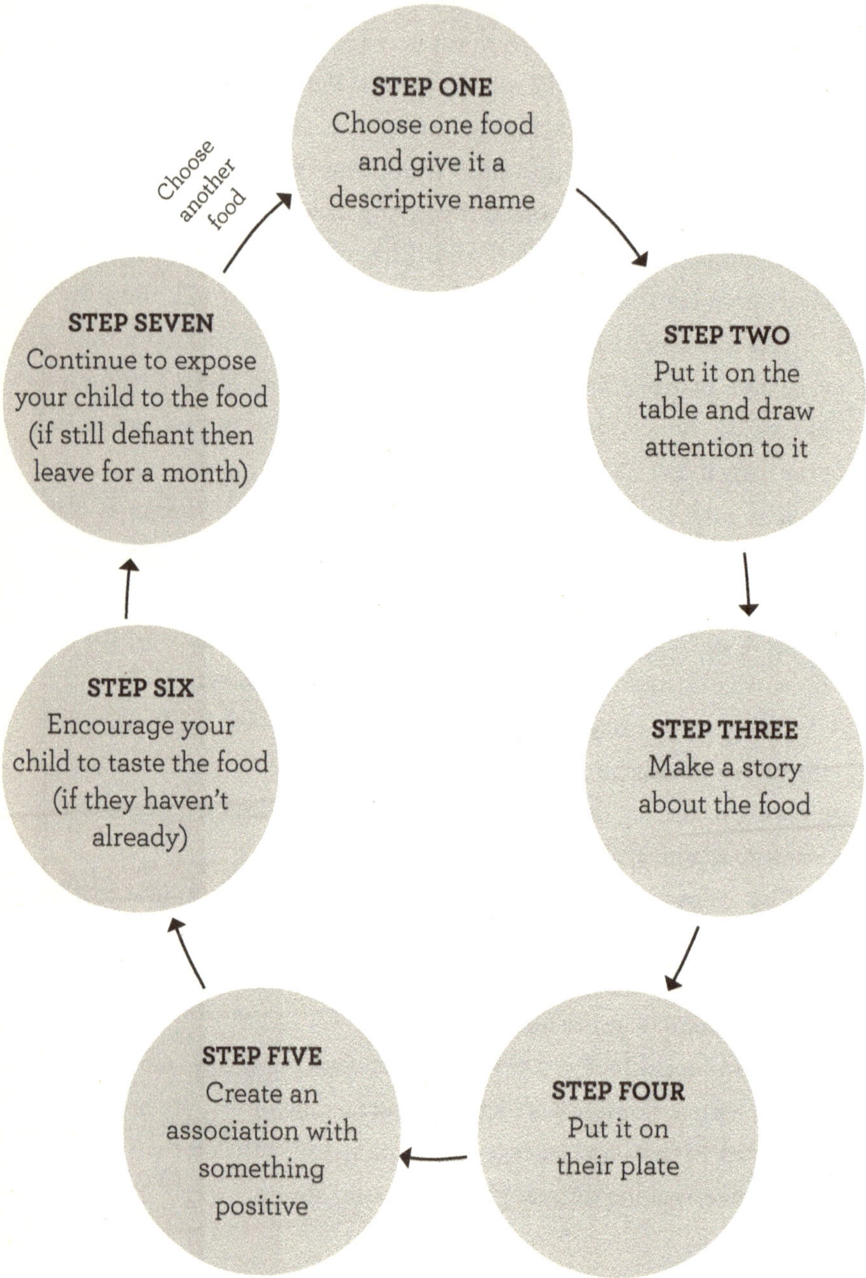

When memorising facts, our brain learns better by repeated exposure or recall. As time passes, more information is memorised if we recall the new information repeatedly.

Therefore, after your child tries a new food for the first time, continue to expose them to it over the following days. After they have tried it three or four nights in a row, start spacing out the exposure, serving it every second, then every third day, etc. They are more likely to form a taste for it by being exposed to it regularly than if you get them to try it once a month.

Tip: Introduce only one food at a time. Choosing more can be overwhelming for you and for your children. See chapter eleven on 'foodication' for the next level in practical advice.

Positive association

American researcher Brian Wansink was trying to understand why some children developed a positive association with healthy foods that were not liked by most children. His team interviewed a couple of hundred three- to five-year-olds.

One surprising finding was that at one daycare centre, all of the children had a strong preference for broccoli, something not seen in other children outside this facility. Most of the children told the researchers they liked it because it was cool.

Intrigued as to why the children thought this, the researchers followed these lines of inquiry and found that the positive association could be traced back to two brothers who attended the centre. These two brothers, who also loved dinosaurs, explained that they liked broccoli because they reminded them of dinosaur trees. They found that the boys' mother had told a story to her children that broccoli looked like dinosaur trees, and that they could pretend they were long-necked dinosaurs eating them. Result: kids who happily ate broccoli.

When encouraging your children to eat, put yourself in their shoes. To say 'Eat it because it will keep you healthy' doesn't work with most adults, so how are children meant to comprehend this? Turn the tables. What do your children like? What are they interested in? Can you make positive associations with a food that will encourage them to eat more of it?

A friend of mine asked her children to help her make a rainbow salad. They went through all the colours of the rainbow and choose vegetables that could go into it — a great positive association.

Make connections

Try seeing eating experiences through your children's eyes. If someone plopped down a food that you had never seen before and encouraged you to eat it because they know you will like it, even the most adventurous person would be dubious. You may know what to expect when someone cooks up teriyaki chicken, but your children do not. Make connections they can understand. 'This is the chicken like we had in the sushi the other day', or 'Grated beetroot is similar to grated carrot, it just makes your tongue go red. Can you get your tongue to go red?'

Progressions

Another way to get children to try a new food is to get them to develop a taste for it without them knowing, like in the spinach/greens progression below or by making associations as they try something new. I did this to help my children form a taste for all nuts and seeds.

Like most children they liked pistachios — breaking them open was a novelty. From pistachios I moved on to sunflower seeds and pumpkin seeds. My children tried them because I said they were like pistachios. Once they were at this stage, I added tamari seasoning[24] and then progressed to cut-up nuts. I have found some children don't like nuts not because of the taste, but more because they are big and the texture is funny to them. They may accept them if you cut them up in a way that feels better for them.

PROGRESSION IDEAS

NUTS

Pistachios → Seeds → Roasted with seasoning (coconut aminos or tamari work well) → Roasted nuts, cut up with seasoning → Mixed raw nuts and seeds

SPINACH/GREENS

Smoothie or purée with added spinach → Cut into small pieces and put in dishes such as meatballs → Put on plate (and follow steps to new food)

Anchoring

If your children are being particularly restrictive in what they want to try, you can use anchoring to your advantage. By putting a large portion of the food (once it is not new) on their plate and saying 'Just one bite', even if they take a small bite, they are starting to train their taste buds. By serving a large portion, the enormity of having one small bite is easier to get their head around than using a small portion and getting them to finish it. You anchor them to the idea of the larger amount, so they are happy to only have to eat a small amount of it.

Anchoring is used as a marketing ploy. At a supermarket or department store they could be selling toilet paper for a reduced price with a sign saying 'LIMIT: FOUR'. You may only need one, you may need none, but the fact that a limit has been set makes you want to buy three or four.

When you want to sell a car or a house, do you list the price you would take? No, you put on a larger price. This way the buyer is anchored at a higher price. In most cases they will offer you a price that is less than your advertised offer, but the initial price sets a standard for negotiations to take place. The person buying will feel that they 'got a deal' when you come down on your original price.

Anchoring, though a bit sneaky, will help your children wrap their head around trying new food. Then it is up to you to create an environment where they don't feel like they have to justify why they don't like it. They have the space to decide for themselves and will more often than not develop a growing appreciation for that food.

IT'S ALL ABOUT FORMING TASTE BUDS

Think about forming taste buds rather than trying to figure out what your children like and dislike. When they don't like something, say something like, 'The more you try it, the more you will like it' or, 'Yeah, you just haven't tried it enough times yet.' I often say this to my children.

Once, we decided to mix it up and get Thai takeaways. I don't normally cook this way or get this sort of takeaway, so it wasn't a surprise when Rasmus piped up, 'I don't like these noodles.' It *was* a surprise (to his grandparents), however, when he continued, 'It's just because I haven't tried them enough times yet.' I realised then just how much of a sponge children are.

Create a habitual mindset in your children that taste buds are trained. That the more they try something, the more they will like it. That the more they try something, the more 'like an adult' they will be. Encourage them to talk openly about their taste preferences and enlist them in trying to figure out if you (or they) can cook or prepare a food in a way that tastes better. You will find they will try more foods without you standing over them, and consequently the variety of food they eat will increase. Trying and eating healthy food will ultimately be an enjoyable experience for them.

ACTION STEPS

Think about taste as a skill to be learnt and not found out. Start by implementing one of the following techniques tonight at dinner time:

1. Use descriptive names for the meal or for individual items on their plate.
2. Talk about a food that they don't like in a positive way, one that means something to your child.
3. Make a connection between one food that they like and another, new food.
4. Start the first step of a progression.
5. Try anchoring.

CHAPTER EIGHT

TAKE IT OR LEAVE IT

When my first child, Huxley, came along, I realised that I wanted to give her more when it came to food. I wanted to give her a healthy relationship with food from the get-go, to carry her right through her teenage and early adult years when many girls struggle with body issues and food intake. Yet I could not rely on my experiences as I was one of the majority who had had all those body issues and consequently food issues.

I had to do some more research. Not in-the-lab research, but real-world stuff, out in the field. Truth be told, I didn't know anyone who had a healthy relationship with food. While some talked about 'going on a diet', some talked about how they were 'naughty' last night and had a dessert, and others, although it seemed like they had a healthy diet, were so wound up about food that anxiety showed on their face when in a social setting. So I started to ask 'What habits around food do you wish you had?' and 'If food wasn't an issue, what would change in your life?' These questions often yielded responses that were gold.

Hunger habits (page 130) and taste buds in training (see page 143) are the foundations in developing a healthy relationship with food. Habits are an 'acquired behaviour that we repeat regularly until it becomes almost involuntary'.[25] These next habits are the top habits most adults wished they had around food.

I see these habits as add-ons in developing a healthy relationship with food. If we raise kids with these habits they will be repeated unconsciously, instead of their relationship with food being a crutch and something they need to change — they will eat what they like when they like, without guilt, shame or any negative emotions. On top of that, the food they will choose to eat will make them feel awesome!

Please note, these next habits are ones which I have identified to be useful in my life and parenting my children. They may not be for everyone, but I have included them here as food for thought.

EATING A VARIETY OF FOOD

Eating a variety of food is important. When you eat a variety of food you don't need to worry about getting enough of specific nutrients. For example, by eating a variety of food, from green leafy vegetables to dairy, your calcium needs will be taken care of. The need to buy calcium-enriched yoghurts won't even cross your mind.

I do realise, however, that you may be starting with a child who won't even change brands of rice, let alone eat a variety of foods. If your children get fussy even when you introduce different brands, then you may feel that introducing more of a variety of foods is not possible. I encourage you to start where you are right now. Start by buying a different brand, then move onto different foods that are similar to what they like and finally progressing to different foods as outlined earlier.

Eating a variety of food is also a great habit to create because then you are decreasing the likelihood of a phenomenon known as habituation. Habituation is when we cease to respond to a given stimulus after repeated presentation. In terms of food this means when we are first given a new food it can be exciting, but after being repeatedly given the same food, say vegetable sticks, habituation can occur and therefore less is eaten. Variety can be simply changing the way you cut or season the food, thus decreasing the chances of the habituation process taking place.

How to create this habit

First of all, I'll repeat: If you are not doing it, you cannot expect your children to do it. Lead the way by experimenting with foods you are not familiar with. Make it a game with your children. Get them to choose a weird-looking vegetable at the supermarket and Google a recipe to try. Getting them involved has a double benefit as they also become involved with preparing the food, instead of eating being a one-way street.

Note: If your child doesn't like to try anything new and also struggles with new situations outside the home, then try to build the 'muscle of trying new things' just by doing new stuff, like going to a different playground, meeting new people, going on a different walk, etc. Remember, behaviours are like a muscle: the more we exercise them, the stronger they get. Getting your child comfortable with doing new things will help with getting comfortable with trying new foods.

HEALTHY SNACKING

Mary ate 'healthy'. Mary was also 100 kg and 1.72 m tall. She ate a great breakfast, brought her lunch to work and prepared mainly salads for dinner. Well-meaning friends and family who saw her eat could not figure out not only why she weighed so much but also why she continued to increase in size each year.

She came to me not really for nutritional advice, but because she ultimately wanted me to justify her obesity with a gene or something that she couldn't control. She was in for a surprise.

When we are not ready to face our situation fully we find excuses or 'memes'[26] to justify why we are the way we are. I was having none of it. After a few sessions, Mary's walls began to tumble down. She started to admit that she did snack — a little bit of ice-cream here, a chocolate bar there, soft drinks 'now and again'. Nothing too out of control, or as she put it, 'Not as bad as most of the people at work'.

I have seen countless people like Mary. They eat healthy, balanced meals. You could say they don't even overeat at mealtimes. Yet snacks make up most of their diet. They are so full up on snacks, they only eat small meals because they are not hungry. The snacks they eat are typical, convenient and mostly unhealthy.

What food do you envision when someone says snack food? Most people respond with chips, biscuits and crackers — all foods where you can open a packet and consume. Convenience food.

When I asked Mary where she had most of her snacks, her reply was in the car, in front of the TV or on the go. She ate snacks when she was distracted. Eating when distracted increases not only the amount you eat but also how much you remember you ate (see page 136 for more on this). At university we studied many papers showing that with obese people there was a discrepancy between what they ate and what they reported they had eaten.

It was, and still is, a common belief that obese individuals lie about how much they eat. This has always bothered me. I was in the field, meeting and interviewing these obese individuals. Like my Dad, I see the best in people. I never believed they were lying to be deliberately deceptive. I knew they wanted to change and were honestly oblivious to the reasons why they seemed to gain weight, when eating 'just like' their skinny friend. I believe that they were telling the truth, their truth. Like Mary, they genuinely didn't remember how much food (and unhealthy food) they actually consumed.

How to create this habit

Make snacks inconvenient. Keep snacks out of sight. When we see food we can become hungry, so keep a clear bench.

Even better, keep biscuits, chips and crackers out of the house. Don't buy them to keep in the house 'just in case'. I am not saying don't ever have these foods, but make them less convenient.

When Ben and I lived in Japan for a period, at first we found buying food at the supermarket a bit daunting. In Japan, the food is completely different, so I got into a habit of not buying any of the traditional snack foods. Also, we didn't have a car, so whenever Ben or I got a craving for something sweet or even felt like a beer, we would have to jump on our bikes and ride for 10 minutes to get whatever we felt like. Talk about inconvenient! Sometimes we would still go, but more often than not the ride in the rain or cold was not worth it. Making traditional snack food not out of bounds but inconvenient will help to decrease distracted snacking.

With children, you can make snacking inconvenient by asking them to put the snack on a plate and have it at the table. Doing this has been an eye-opener for me. In the past, the children have just taken a snack and eaten as they played or watched a movie, often eating for eating's sake. When they have to sit down to eat a snack, they will only snack if they are actually hungry.

Snacks don't have to be chips, crackers or biscuits. Make a habit that snacks are 'real food' — fruit, nuts, vegetables, hummus, etc. This is easier to create as a habit when children are small than to change children's snacks when they are older. But it can still be done. A friend of mine started to clean up her diet, and as a by-product her sons' diet changed as well. She said that it took about two weeks for her sons to stop asking for their snack bars, with the first three days being the worst. If everyone had the habit of snacking on real food, then snacking would become less of an issue in people's lives.

A note on pre-dinner snacks

I am not sure how many times I have started to cook and the children have come into the kitchen saying 'I'm hungry', in that drawn-out, nasal tone. Even when I say, 'Great! Dinner is not far off', sometimes they are not satisfied with this answer and say, 'But I am hungry *now*!'

Thinking of food increases hunger. Smelling food increases hunger. Although I know they think they are starving, chances are they are not.

If you find yourself in this situation try these two things. One, use it as an opportunity to talk about where they feel hunger and what sensations they feel. Doing this helps children to identify real hunger versus false hunger, as mentioned in chapter six. Also, you can use it to increase vegetable consumption. Before you start to cook, cut some vegetable sticks (carrots, celery, cucumber, capsicum). When the smell of cooking wafts through the house and your children come hunting for food, you are prepared.

Although this can reinforce the habit of snacking before dinner, if you say you can only eat real food before dinner, their habit of snacking pre-dinner will be on healthy stuff, not filling up on crackers or other processed food.

STARTING THE DAY RIGHT

How you start the day has a knock-on effect on how the whole day goes. When you wake up in a grumpy mood, you will kick your shin against the bed, spill your hot drink over yourself and trip over a toy — all before you get out your door. The world seems to conspire against you when you start the day in a grump.

What you eat first thing in the morning has the same effect. If you eat an unhealthy breakfast, chances are you will continue to eat unhealthily all day. If you eat a sugar-laden breakfast you will set yourself up to have a day of 'the battle of willpower', because of the subsequent sugar highs, sugar lows and sugar cravings.

Growing up with a habit of 'starting the day right' — an unconscious belief that you need to start the day well — will help your children to choose healthier food during the day. Others will be getting a sugar low at 10am and craving a chocolate bar, but your grown child will very rarely, if ever, get these cravings.

Starting the day well, with a healthy choice of food, will help your children to continue to choose healthy options during the day. It also gives you an excuse for not eating sweet food in the morning.

Once, it was about 8.30am and I decided to go and do the supermarket shopping. The children had woken up particularly early that morning and it felt more like midday than 8.30am! (I am sure you have had one of 'those days'.) As we entered the supermarket, Huxley spotted a girl eating a chocolate bar. Her innocent comment was, 'Look, Mum, she is eating chocolate', said in a way that suggested she was thinking, 'I didn't know you could do that.' It was a very unusual sight for her to see someone eating chocolate so early in the morning. It got me thinking. What time have I unconsciously taught my children that it is okay to eat sweets? When do I think it is okay? We all grow up with different beliefs and I had one that my parents, knowingly or not, had suggested: that eating sweets for breakfast was just not done. Come to think about it, if I am offered even a muffin before 10am I think twice . . .

This is where I think the lines get a bit blurry. Keeping the end — instilling a healthy relationship with food — in sight, I think it is okay to be slightly rigid in this area, especially when your children are really young.

How to create this habit

To instil this habit, you need to work out what is a healthy start to the day. Everyone will have different views on this. Your children's views will change as they grow up and get exposed to different cultures and experiences. However, if they grow up with the habit of starting the day right they are more likely to choose food that makes them feel good. Also, when they learn more about food and what is good for them, they will be more likely to develop secondary habits to enforce the 'starting your day right' habit. For example, they may learn that drinking 600 ml of water with the juice of one lemon in it is a great start to the day. They are more likely to form the habit of having water with lemon juice if they have the mindset of starting your day right.

Starting your day right, combined with the hunger habit of checking-in (see page 133), will also have the added benefit of your children becoming aware which breakfast works for them. Remember, one man's food is another man's poison. By having the habit of starting the day right and then checking-in as the day progresses, they will come to realise what exactly 'starting the day right' means for them.

Growing up on a dairy farm, my father would milk the cows at 5am and come back home at 8am for a big fry-up breakfast of eggs, farm-fresh bacon, beans and black pudding. I was interested in nutrition even in my early teens; I didn't know much but I accepted commonly held beliefs about what you 'should' eat and I was concerned for my father, who in my eyes was eating himself into heart disease. I asked him once if eating cereal or even porridge wouldn't be better for him. I have never forgotten his response: 'If I eat that, I will be hungry at 10am. Eating this breakfast lasts me to 2pm, when I can have a light lunch that will set me right until after the night milking.' I am still in awe that my father, who didn't make it past the equivalent of year 10 at school, had a solid grip on how food made him feel. He is one of the most active, healthy 65-year-olds that I know!

To start the day right, you need to set the environment. You might like to start the day with happy music — after all, happy people choose healthier food. Start conversations with your children, asking them how the food makes them feel, and how long it took for them to get hungry when eating eggs on toast as opposed to sugary cereal.

In New Zealand, reading is taught to children with as much emphasis on comprehension as actually reading the words correctly. The same goes with food. It is more about their comprehension that eating sugary cereal will make them feel hungry before long, or even grumpy, while oats or eggs will fill them up until morning-tea time and make them feel energised throughout the morning.

Start the conversation and allow the comprehension to happen over time. See the Appendix (page 232) for a form that you can use to help teach children to comprehend starting the day right.

Have you ever noticed that you sometimes say to your children what your parents have said to you? It is said that our parents' voices become our inner voices. Develop a one-line phrase that instils a habit of starting the day right. For example, if your children ask for chocolate or cake for breakfast, have a standard reply such as, 'Oh, we need to start the day right before we have cake.' It is not too much of a biggie in terms of *what* you say, but more *how* you say it. If the request is met with a rigid 'No', they may feel like they are being deprived. Deprivation just increases their craving and they are more likely to sneak this food later. If the phrase is said in an upbeat, open tone but in a no-room-for-argument way, that is what your children will start to believe — you always start the day right!

When you travel around or stay at other people's houses you don't always have the food that you may think starts the day well. I have seen some parents get their knickers in a twist because their children are not eating as well as they normally do. I have done this myself. The result is an unhappy environment and therefore unhappy children — not starting the day right, and quite the opposite of what you want.

When travelling and outside of your normal daily routine it is a time to be open as a parent. Your children are not going to have your ideal breakfast at times. Once you accept this you can turn it into a learning experience. Chances are, if the options for your children are not healthy, the options for you are not going to be healthy either. Create an open conversation with your children about how you ate toast with honey for breakfast this morning and you don't feel as energised as you do when you have your eggs and avocado (or whatever your go-to is). The trick is to talk about *your* experience. Just like when we start talking about our experience to other adults, they will start talking about their experience. Your children will start, if not talking about their experiences, at least thinking about them.

Instil the habit of starting the day right. Make it a habit that your whole family does, just like it is a habit that you go toilet before bed. It will become a subconscious habit that your children will take with them into their adult life — a habit that will set them up to have a healthy relationship with food.

NOT EATING AFTER DINNER

I can hear the sighs now. A number of times I have suggested this to people who struggle with food and I can see their agitation. Their eyes glaze over and their body tenses up. Give up eating after dinner? What, no dessert? Nobody does that!

While this definitely may not be for you, first let me explain why I think it is a good habit to get into. If you always offer dessert after dinner, what does this teach your children? You end the night eating something sweet.

While I think this is okay once in a while, to do it every night and feel as if you have to have something sweet after dinner is not a healthy relationship with food. It becomes a craving or a habitual response. It controls you.

I have recently spent time at my parents' place. Dessert is always served, and as all of my sisters were there with their kids, I didn't make an issue over it. But having dessert every night, even though it was just one week, created a habit. After leaving my parents' and going to my in-laws', where dessert is not offered, my daughter said after dinner one night, 'Nana, can I have some ice-cream? I feel like something sweet.' It is amazing how quickly habits are created in children.

But never fear, it is also amazing how quickly habits can be broken. Creating a habit of not eating after dinner will become an unconscious choice, just as having a snack after dinner is an unconscious choice for most.

Although I didn't grow up with this habit of not eating after dinner, I have created this habit for myself and I now find it weird when people start eating after dinner. I unconsciously think, 'Why are they eating? Did they not eat enough for dinner?' By making a habit of not eating after dinner, your children will grow up with this being normal for them. If they ever feel as though dinner has not satisfied them and they want something else to eat, then make it real food, like fruit, vegetables or nuts. Leave sweet desserts, cookies, etc. for the odd occasion.

How to create this habit

I use the phrase, 'Are you satisfied? Remember, we don't eat until breakfast.' Remember that your voice will become your children's inner voice. Saying 'This is the last meal of the day', in a matter-of-fact tone, will create this go-to in their head.

If children do not eat what you think is enough, trust them, but keep the dinner out. Say to them, 'Okay, I can see you're not hungry. I am not too sure if you have had enough, so I will keep your dinner here, just in case you get hungry later on.' When they have finished their dinner and they are still not satisfied, offer some fruit. If they are always asking for fruit after dinner, add a serving of fruit to dinner.

You can also do this with dessert-like items. Having ice-cream as a part of dinner sounds counter-intuitive, but it only sounds that way because you have a belief that ice-cream is a treat, or maybe it was used to reward you for finishing your dinner. By having the dessert *with* dinner you are making a point that it is just another food item, no more or no less good than the dinner. It is teaching your children a different point of view — one that you, like me, may have trouble seeing, but then that is your belief and not a fact.

If you are like me and really cannot bring yourself to serve a sweet item at dinner time, then make a healthy alternative but call it by its mainstream name. For years my children thought ice-cream was always blended frozen banana and frozen strawberries, because they knew no different. But when other children spoke of ice-cream they could relate, or at least they thought they could.

Other ways to help break the habit of eating sweet things after dinner is to brush your children's teeth straight after dinner. This becomes a habit, and signals the end of eating for the day. I also used this method to help break my habit of eating sweets after dinner. It gives you an enforced pause, and eating after brushing your teeth always tastes horrible.

Not eating after dinner may be the biggest habit for you to wrap your head around, probably because you don't think you can do it. My advice is this, you don't think you can do it because you have grown up with the belief that you have to eat something after dinner, even if it is fruit salad. It is probably a way to treat yourself.

You don't need it: it is just a belief that has turned into a habit that has turned into a craving. Like Pavlov's dog salivating when it heard a bell, your body starts to give you signals that you need to eat something more at the end of the day. You don't.

PLEASURE FROM EATING

Savour your food. Taste your food. Eat for pleasure. When you savour food, you eat slower, you eat more mindfully, you eat less and you eat better-quality food.

As discussed earlier, many people have the mentality that food is an enemy: that you need to keep reminding yourself that you 'should eat' certain things because they are healthy; that you 'shouldn't eat' other things because it will cause you to gain weight. It becomes a battle. Even when we are eating healthily, thoughts such as, 'Am I eating all the colours?', 'Is there enough variety here?', 'Should I have cooked that broccoli less?' all creep in.

When I suggest eating for pleasure, most parents would say, 'If I taught that to my children, all they would choose to eat is cupcakes and chicken nuggets.' Maybe that is because you don't trust yourself with food, so you don't trust your children either.

Create a habit of enjoying a meal. Eating because you get pleasure out of the different tastes and experiences is the foundation on which a healthy relationship with food is built. By establishing a belief that eating should be an enjoyable experience, you are instilling a relationship with food that becomes conscious. You eat food because you enjoy the experience it offers.

Enjoying eating will foster a relaxing eating atmosphere. When we are stressed our digestion is affected, so although we might be eating healthy foods, we are not fully digesting and assimilating them. By creating a joyful experience with food, you and your children will be better off not only because they ate that healthy food but because they were able to digest and assimilate it better as well.

How to create this habit

Creating an enjoyable eating experience starts with you. Your energy around meal times is crucial. You being relaxed teaches your children to be relaxed around food. Meeting their needs with warmth rather than fixed, rigid boundaries will increase their enjoyment of eating (see pages 107 and 148 for more on meeting children's needs with warmth).

You can take it one step further and have fun with cooking and experimenting with different food (see the next chapter for ideas about getting your children involved with this). For example, you can make smiley faces out of food or look at the beautiful way the Japanese present food. These things make food fun and more appealing to eat.

Learn to trust your children with food. Don't have any 'restricted' food in your house. If you cannot bring yourself to have chocolate as an anytime food or for eating after real food, then don't have it in your home. This way you can treat all food as just food — none better or worse than any other, none restricted. Take away the rewards, bribes, punishment and guilt attachment to food.

Throughout the last three chapters I have outlined habits that I think, and many other people believe, help to create a healthy relationship with food. But the reality is that you are coming from a different background to me, and have different circumstances. It is my intention throughout this book not to tell you what to do, but to arm you with information and increase your awareness about food. Think about what habits you want to commit to creating in your children. Food affects everyone's lives whether we like it or not, so we may as well empower ourselves, therefore empowering our children.

ACTION STEPS

This is where you get to decide what you want for your children and what habits you want to create. It is the crux of this book.

A Chinese proverb is: 'Tell me, I forget. Show me, I remember. Involve me, I understand.' Even if you have not completed the Action Steps prior to this one, do not skip this one. It will help you get clear in your own head what you want, and therefore make it easier to put it into action in your children's lives. There are no right or wrong answers, by the way, just whatever you want for your family.

1. Sit down with your partner and discuss what you want for your children around food. Are you okay with processed food for every snack, or do you want to put real food first, or something in-between?
2. Is going to McDonald's/cafés/takeaways a once-a-week outing, once a month, or not at all?
3. Discuss and list what habits you think would help your children develop a healthy relationship with food.
4. Look at your list. What do you need to do in order to encourage your children to do this, i.e. if you have hunger habits as a part of your list, how will you explain being satisfied and hunger levels? How can you remember to keep asking your children about their hunger?
5. Look at your list again. Are there any situations where instilling these habits will become an issue? Develop a plan to handle this, e.g. snacking

sitting down — when you are at someone else's place and their friends do not sit down to snack, do you enforce this or explain that other people have different rules in their home? Or when other kids come to your house and want to play while eating, will you explain gently that in your home you sit down to snack, or will you let it slide when friends are over? (Again, there are no right or wrong answers — everyone will be different. What is important here is to remain consistent with what you do.)

PART III

Let's Get Dirty

CHAPTER NINE

CREATING AUTONOMY

I have seen many children go through a door-opening and -closing stage. They must open and close the door themselves — not an adult, not their big brothers. *Them*. They throw a tantrum when someone else opens or closes the door.

I have seen many parents meet these needs if they are not in a hurry. They let the child open and close the door. The parents give them that experience. When they fight it, they always lose!

How can we be the same parent who lets them open the door as many times as they like when it comes to eating? The thought of someone ordering for me at a restaurant without my consent makes me want to hurl. To not be asked what I want to eat seems wrong to me. I want that autonomy over my food choices. I want to experience how my decisions — good or bad — affect me.

Children are no different. As soon as we do things that say 'I don't trust you', like making them eat everything on their plate or saying 'You will eat all of your vegetables — or else', you take away their autonomy and they learn not to trust their instincts around food. This leads to children who are influenced by external cues to eat rather than their own internal cues.

Creating autonomy in children starts, firstly, with you opening the lines of communication and, secondly, getting them involved. Give them some control. Create an environment where they feel safe sharing their opinions on food — just like you do when you allow them to open and close the door all by themselves.

THE INITIAL CONVERSATION

Having read this far, you have probably started to shift gears and are changing how you are interacting with your children at mealtimes. With not-so-good results?

Here's the thing: you are reading this book and getting ideas of how things could be better. You can see that trying to control your children in the past has not worked, so you are starting to try something new. You are excited about this and it feels good.

But your children don't know this — they did not get the memo. They are used to you saying, 'Eat all your dinner, then you will get dessert.' So they eat everything on their plate, but now they are not getting any dessert after dinner. What?

Sit down and talk with your children, even if they are very young and you don't think they will understand. There is no magical age that children get to and then automatically comprehend what you are talking about — it happens over time.

I remember always guiding Huxley to get off the bed backwards. She was very young when I started saying 'go off backwards' repeatedly, while showing her how. One day when she was just eight months old (she was an early mover) I was on the other side of the room when I saw her move to get off the bed. I started saying 'go off backwards', while walking towards her to guide her. To my surprise, she turned around and did it herself. Before that day I was not sure she was actually listening to me, let alone understanding what I was saying. This experience showed me that children comprehend more than we give them credit for.

Sit down and talk to your children in a way that they are likely to understand. Whatever you say, make sure you back it up with what you do. For example, if you say you are not going to pressure them to clean their plates to get dessert, you have to put the effort in to follow through.

NO PRESSURE

Being open and non-judgemental will help to keep the communication lines open with your children. This can be especially important at the dinner table.

I have experienced this first hand. I have been a bit of a martyr in the past when it came to mealtimes: putting effort into cooking and expecting my children to be grateful for what I had done. When they haven't been grateful or have been particularly *ungrateful*, I haven't responded that nicely. Even if it was an accepted phrase such as, 'You don't have to like it but you do have to try it', it was said through gritted teeth.

Then I put being open and receptive into the forefront of my mind, accepting that the children were entitled to have their own opinions on food. I came up with phrases and techniques I could use to encourage them to keep an open mind to food, even if they didn't like it at the time.

I remember the first meal after I 'changed my tune'. I had cooked something new and I wasn't too sure they would like it. My son, who was two at the time, registered his disgust. I then opened up the conversation with, 'Did you try some?'

'No,' he said.

'Well, what do you think you will not like about it? Can you suggest a way that it will taste better?'

I took a line of being inquisitive. I thought if I knew what he was willing to try, I could work out how I could make it a more pleasing experience for him.

The first time I did that, I was amazed at how he sat quietly for awhile and then after talking about the day, he started to eat happily. Later on, he said in his own words how proud he was of himself that he had tried it, because he did really like it.

Since this first encounter, I have continued to set an open, receptive tone. Sometimes my children will try something and say they like it, other times they still may say yuck. What I have found really interesting is that sometimes they turn around and say, 'Actually, I tried it enough times and I like it now.'

We all see the world through different eyes. Just because when I look at a grated beetroot and carrot salad I see aliveness, something that I know will make me feel good, doesn't mean that my son feels this way. I can be fixed and rigid, trying to persuade him to adopt my point of view. I am sure you have all had a 'conversation', a.k.a. argument, with someone who just didn't share your point of view. No matter how much you think you're right, you just can't seem to get through to them. Children are the same. We can miss the chance to see the world through their eyes and consequently miss the opportunity to foster a love of healthy food.

One day, when I opened up a conversation about how I could cook different vegetables in ways that they would like, and asked my children what would help them to want to eat their broccoli, I saw how my past reactions had scared my eldest child. She, too, didn't like the look of the meal that night, but she didn't want to say so, because she was scared she was going to hurt my feelings.

It was one of those moments where you realise with a pang that what you have done in the past has really affected your children, and not for the good. In line with being honest and open with her, I said, 'Yep, I haven't reacted that well in the past, Huxley. But I am trying to be better. How about we go through some recipe books and you can tell me what you like the look of?' She really perked up and was excited that she would get an opportunity to choose her own meals, rather than get them dictated to her.

Becoming open and non-judgemental has created a better dinner-table experience. Dinner times have become not only more pleasurable, but I have learnt a lot about what foods my children like, and why. From the texture to the seasoning, their replies continue to increase, just because I became inquisitive and started listening.

Develop a positive conversation around meals. If your children are being particularly rigid, then just talk about something other than the food in front of them. For example, you could ask what their favourite part of the day was, or you could start a conversation about what foods they think Superman likes. As soon as you try to encourage them to eat something specific, you may lose their interest and they may not try it — not because they don't want to, but to prove that they are right. Being non-judgemental and open to their feelings and what they say will provide an environment where they feel it is safe to try more food. It will create a positive association with food, maybe not now but in the future.

The element of surprise

I learned something else interesting when I was looking for different things to put in my children's lunchboxes. I would send a few things that they liked and one thing that they had not tried before. It always came back uneaten. It seemed that new food was never eaten at school.

I started to introduce these same foods at home, using the steps outlined on page 156. Once I introduced these foods at home, they would be eaten from the kids' lunchboxes.

Most people are more likely to stick with what they know. How often do you order something new at a restaurant? It is no wonder then that children will eat what they know first from their school lunchbox. If you like to surprise your children with food, don't! But make serving food and trying new food an open conversation and experience.

WHEN YOU KNOW THEIR IDEAS ARE NOT THEIR IDEAS

Your child comes home and announces that their much-loved seaweed snack is 'yuck'. You probe and get told that a child at school said their snack looked like they are eating plastic, and all the other children laughed.

When something like this happens, sit down and have a conversation with your child. See if you can come to an agreement where both your needs (the habits you want to instil) and their needs (not being the uncool kid at school) can be met. These situations are the perfect times to teach your children that everyone is different and that they don't need to be like anyone else. Being able to laugh with them and agree *and eat it anyway* takes courage, something that many adults wish they had, but comes with practice.

ACTION STEPS

Sit down and talk with your children about food. Tell them how you have reacted in the past and how it hasn't worked. Tell them you want to try a different way to encourage them to have healthy eating habits, as you see that what you have done in the past is not working for them (with specifics if necessary). Tell them how you are just learning yourself, but you want to create habits that you wish you had or that will serve them well as adults, etc. What language you use will depend on their age.

GET THEM INVOLVED

Two-year-old tantrums: you have either been through them, are going through them or have heard about them. The terrible twos. Lots of yelling, clenched fists, and either running on the spot or kicking the floor.

We all accept that they are part of a child's development, but why do they occur? From my own experience, it is because the children want to feel heard and respected and quite often they want to do everything themselves.

When my first daughter was going through this stage I read a book called *The Happiest Toddler on the Block,*[27] which I would recommend to any parent of a toddler. The biggest take-home I got from this book, which changed the way I interacted with my daughter, was to justify her wants. To give an example, if she wants to stay and play at a playground and you need to get going, instead of reacting to her tantrum by ordering her out, repeat what she wants: 'You want to stay, you want to stay.' You keep repeating what she wants until she calms down. At that point, you explain why you cannot stay and possibly give a solution like, 'We will come back tomorrow morning.' If she starts crying again, repeat it again: 'You want to stay, you are having so much fun, you don't want to go.' You do it for as long as it takes to get her attention. Again, explain why you cannot stay and just repeat this until she calms down.

Although it doesn't work 100 per cent of the time, it is amazing how often this does work. You just need to get over the fact that you may look like a nut-job to other parents or passers-by by saying the same sentence over and over again!

I learnt from this that children just want to be heard. They want their feelings and their wants justified — not necessarily given in to, but justified. Getting them involved in the process of cooking, preparing, naming or anything else to do with food helps them to feel like they are contributing, like they have a say.

What follows are some ideas for getting the children involved with mealtimes — directly putting the ball into your children's court, so to speak. Don't think you have to do them all and get them all right. It's like when I try to clean my house — I get my knickers in a twist and get stressed out if I haven't done it all. When I think of having a 'clean' house, I am thinking of *all* the cleaning I need to do. It's a huge job, and even if I get three-quarters of it done I feel like I have not achieved anything. However, when I think of having a 'cleaner' house, even if it is just getting one bathroom or one toilet cleaned, I feel so much better. I feel like I have achieved something. A small change in my mindset, but a much happier self! Keep this in mind when thinking about how you could get your children involved. Just do what feels good for you.

Planting

If you have a vege garden, mark off a section of it and let the children plant whatever they like, in whatever fashion they like. You can try teaching them how to do it 'right', but if they are not interested, then leave them to it. They will soon listen more carefully, when your plants sprout and theirs don't!

If you do not have any space for a garden where you live, then just get a few small herb pots. Your kids can choose the herbs and pick them whenever they feel like having that herb in their meals.

Preparing

Cook with your children. The mere thought of this sends shivers down my spine! As I said, I am a 'why walk when you can run?' type of person. To have to take an hour to cook the evening meal, rather than the 20 minutes it would normally take, was very challenging for me. So if I can do this, you can do it, too!

I think of preparing a meal with my children to be an invaluable experience. Children eventually leave your house and they will be cooking many meals at some stage in their life. By cooking with your children, you are not only teaching them life skills, but you also have the opportunity to show them how to experiment with food and taste new food. Done in a calm, relaxed way, they will develop positive associations with cooking. Imagine if everyone in the world had this experience growing up!

Let them experiment

Although you may not think a sandwich with cheese, sauce, peanut butter and jam sounds good, if your children ever ask you for it, indulge them. You can create boundaries by saying, 'Okay, let's try a little one and see if you like it. If you do, I'll make you a bigger one.' You can also let them 'perform the experiment'.

Huxley went through a stage of making juice. She started off making orange juice by squeezing an orange. She then moved on to banana juice, consisting of mashing up small bits of banana in some water. I wanted so dearly to say, 'What you need to do is mash up the banana and then . . .' but I held back.

The sheer delight that she got from making up her own concoctions was a pleasurable experience. If your children show interest in experimenting, leave them to it and then once they are done, if they don't seem pleased with the result, ask questions such as 'How do you think we can make it better for next time?'

Menus

Ask your children what they want to eat. I am not talking about asking them casually what they want to eat over the next week. I am talking about getting a recipe book — one with lots of pictures — that has loads of recipes you want to try. Then ask your children to go through the book with you and mark what dishes they would like to try. When I first did this with my children, their eyes lit up and they were soon requesting dishes that I had previously thought they wouldn't like! When I decided to cook it, I would talk during the day about how we were going to have the curry they chose and sure enough, when dinner rolled around they were trying it, no questions asked.

Give them a choice

You can create a sense of autonomy by giving your children a choice of what to eat. Instead of saying, 'What shall we eat?', pick several meal options and ask them what they would prefer. Shall we have cucumber or broccoli tonight? Or even, shall we have rice-paper wraps or roast chicken? You define the boundaries, yet they feel empowered because they get a choice.

Rasmus would always turn his nose up at capsicums. One day I asked him, 'We have green, yellow, red and orange capsicums — which one would you like?' For the next three months he ate yellow capsicums. Although I think the different colours taste pretty similar, he only wanted yellow ones. After a while he started adding in the other colours. Instead of insisting he eat capsicums, I gave him a choice — a choice that as adults we might not feel is that big a deal, but for children it is huge.

Develop a food critic

Develop a habit of putting out 'tasting menus', comprised of small, bite-size portions of new foods. Get your children to taste the food, ask if they like it or how they would like it better, etc. This is a great strategy, as it teaches them to try new food, but it also teaches them that people are entitled to different opinions (see chapter eleven).

If you have children who are really afraid of new food, especially real food, then start by offering processed food, work your way to now-and-again food and eventually up to real food, or just mix it up (see page 110 for definitions of these food levels).

Take them to the supermarket

Thinking about taking three children to the supermarket, you might say, 'Oh no, why would you?' Answer: because there is food there.

Going down the aisles that contain chocolates, desserts, etc, is a recipe for disaster, so keep your shopping journey to the perimeter of the supermarket, where the real food is displayed. You will get to go past all the fruit and vegetables with them. Ask them to help you pick out the best-looking apples and other produce. Get them to pick one vegetable or fruit they want to try. Get them excited about eating real food and about trying different food and experimenting with ways to eat it.

FALL-BACK

If you are a parent whose children are very picky eaters who often refuse to eat dinner, you may even spend extra time preparing other food, just so they will eat at all. If you find yourself trying to get your children to eat a variety of food, yet it is a continual battle of wills, the 'fall-back' option could be an answer.

The fall-back is having one food option (no cooking required) that is always there for your children to request if they don't want to eat the dinner you have prepared. It needs to be a food you know they will eat, but they will have to consider if they want to give up their dinner for that food. It needs to be a food they like, not love, and it must be the same all the time.

This way you are still giving your children autonomy over their food choices. When they don't want to eat the dinner you have cooked, and when the fall-back food stays the same, chances are they will get bored of it after a while and think twice about giving up their hot, freshly cooked dinner for their fall-back option.

Get your child to help you choose which food is their fall-back, putting the ball in their court — but once they have made up their mind, don't switch just because they don't want it anymore.

I read about the fall-back option in *It's Not About the Broccoli* by Dina Rose. (She writes about using cottage cheese in this way with her child and how that worked very well. See her website itsnotaboutnutrition.squarespace.com for more information.) Truthfully, initially I thought it was a permissive idea. However, I don't have a problem with my children not eating dinner and going to bed hungry — I have found they will only do that once. Yet I have heard other parents saying their children will not eat day after day if they don't give them something they like to eat at dinner. I have also had parents say that their children will not sleep if they did not eat anything at dinner times.

All children and parents are different. The fall-back may fit into your family when you are looking at ways to get your children to eat dinner but are tired of preparing other meals when they turn up their noses at what you cook.

You don't need to do everything in this chapter, just choose one thing that is realistic for you to do and start there. I remember the first time I got the kids to help with cutting up vegetables for dinner — my gosh, it took a long time! However, I found that by changing my head space into 'Okay, this is teaching them some great skills and lessons', I was able to help them explore more instead of thinking how slow the meal preparation was going.

When we get children to help with food, quite often the first step is changing our head space, *then* getting them involved. To change your headspace, just think about the bigger picture. When we come from a space of 'what habits will this teach them?', or 'what can they learn from this?', it is easier to help them and be in the moment of teaching them about healthy foods and enjoying the process along the way.

ACTION STEPS

There are so many ways to get your children involved with food, and as a consequence to develop autonomy around food. The important thing is to make it fun for them. Done right, you can even bond over healthy food.

What can you do today to get them involved with eating? Choose one of the above ways to help them get involved and write down the steps you will need to take to implement this. Doing one small step each day doesn't make it so overwhelming.

For example, planting with children:

1. Create a list of reasons why you want to plant with your children.
2. Write down a list of things you will need.
3. Set aside a time to go to the store and choose seeds, etc.
4. Set a time to plant with your children.
5. Are there any lessons along the way you want to draw their attention to? — how you water the plant, how you don't disturb it, the names of the plants, etc.

Note: Remember what is was like the first time you saw a plant sprouting from a seed. This will help you to create a sense of awe and excitement when explaining it to your children.

CHAPTER TEN

TASTICATION

'My children just won't eat those healthy foods.' I was sitting at a new friend's place while we watched our children play, and the topic of conversation had turned to food. This was not the first time I had heard a parent say this, but on this day I really heard it.

I thought about this comment for the rest of the day. Knowing what I knew about food and what I have shared with you throughout this book, something didn't quite sit right with me. Yet I was faced with the reality that I, too, believed this. While I gave my kids mostly healthy food, and they were most likely the kids in the playground eating the food that other kids would not, I had a flashback to a situation where I saw a three-year-old eating a roast vegetable salad for lunch. My thought was exactly the same: 'If I gave my children that for lunch, they would not eat it.' It was another 'aha' moment for me, like when I saw that four-year-old eating a whole tomato (see page 29). What is interesting about having an awareness around food and beliefs around food is that it opens you up to everyday situations and how you as a parent can grow from them.

Also at this time, my son started to say 'yuck, vegetables' every time I mentioned them. I digested these two experiences and asked myself: How can I teach older kids who have an aversion to vegetables (or any food) to be open to it? Teaching kids about taste buds in training was a first step but it was proving to be not enough. I needed a way to hammer the message home.

I came up with tastication, and the technique in the next chapter, foodication. Tastication and foodication are both techniques for taste and food education, and are a practical way to further educate children about food.

It has been shown that adults who are 'foodies' or adventurous eaters have better health outcomes than those who are not. Tastication and foodication are a way to develop children into 'foodies', a way to get them involved in their eating and create positive associations with healthy food.

Before we get into the nitty-gritty of tastication and foodication, we need to set the scene. What is important for you to hold in your mind when putting this system in place is the intended outcome — the goals of this system. Just like we have talked about earlier, it is about the bigger picture. Start with the bigger picture and then the details will take care of themselves.

GOALS

When I first drew up the plan for tastication and foodication, I wanted to make sure everything I did was in line with the bigger picture. These are the goals I had in mind when starting this nutrition education programme:

- to help children develop a positive association with real food
- to exercise children's 'trying new food' muscle
- to always follow the mantra 'taste buds in training'
- to develop foodies
- to encourage children to make up their own minds about the taste of food
- to encourage children to think about different ways to cook or make food better
- to encourage children to appreciate different aspects of food: texture, temperature, juiciness, etc
- to open children's awareness that people are different and can have different taste preferences — not wrong or right, just different.

Important note

Although this technique will help your children develop a taste and preference for liking healthy foods, that is not the goal. The intention is to make it fun. If and when it gets overwhelming for you or testing in any way, stop and try it another time in the future. The primary goal here is *positive association*, and this starts with you.

TASTICATION

Tastication is a taste education. It is about teaching our children about taste buds and includes how we train our taste buds, as well as looking at the different taste buds on our tongue. This may be an education for you as well!

Step 1: Taste buds in training

If you need to review taste buds in training, do so now in chapter seven. The starting point for children is understanding that their taste buds are still in training. Although they may not like some foods now, their taste buds will grow — just like their bodies will grow. To help their taste buds grow they will need to keep trying the food, even if it is just a tiny morsel.

This step is about setting the foundations. It is not going to happen after one conversation.

Don't forget to use stories about you and your experiences. I always tell a story to my children about how I didn't like avocado when I was young. I could see my mum (their grandmother) loved it, and I could not work out why. I just didn't like the texture and I thought it tasted funny. However, I started to try it. First I had it as a topping to Marmite on toast and I found the texture was just like that of bananas. Although I didn't fall in love with it straight away, I kept having just a bite of my sister's and gradually moved up to having a whole piece. Then I started to have it with eggs on toast. After many times of trying it, it is now one of my favourite foods and I wish I had started trying it earlier in my life.

As you may have noticed, I also love making the analogy between muscles or bodies and taste buds. Children have an awareness that they cannot do some things adults or even older children can do. Yet they know that when they get to be that older kid, they will be able to do them. Take jumping and hopping, for example. At around the age of two children start to be able to jump with two feet coming off the ground, then at about age three they can start to be able to hop on one foot. Just because they could walk doesn't mean they could jump, and just because they could jump doesn't mean they could hop. It's a progression.

Liking vegetables or new foods is exactly the same. When we first try them, we may not like them, but if we keep trying our taste buds develop just like our bodies develop, until one day we really like the food, just like we will learn to hop on one leg.

Create an analogy or story that means something to your children. Make it a given that your taste buds will develop and that, just like hopping, liking new foods is a badge of honour that shows they are getting older!

Develop your own story that resonates with your child about how taste buds are in training and they need to try foods often to develop a taste for them.

Step 2: Taste bud explanation

This is where you get to sit down with your children and teach them about their taste buds. On the next page is a drawing of a tongue and where the taste buds of each of the basic tastes are concentrated. Help them to make a connection between what foods are sweet and salty by asking them about different foods. 'What do you think a banana tastes like?' (Sweet, salty, sour, bitter, or even encourage them to use their own words at this stage — like cardboard or the beach, etc.) 'Where on the tongue are you likely to taste it?' They may not fully comprehend yet what each taste is like, but you can get them thinking about it.

Spend some time looking at this diagram and then maybe get them to look at their tongue in a mirror, identifying the areas of the tongue that will pick up the different tastes.

THE TONGUE

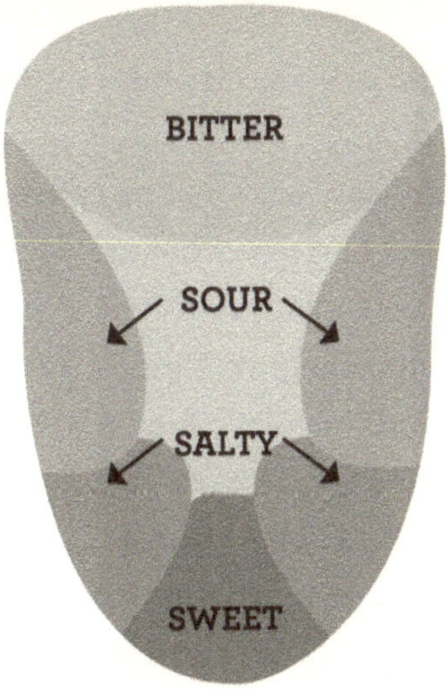

Step 3: Experimentation

This is where the fun really happens for your children.

After going through steps one and two, your children should have a picture in their minds that taste buds are trained through repeated exposure, as well as where the taste buds are found on the tongue. Step three is about letting them experiment for themselves.

Determine if they want to do all the tastes at once or just do one tasting at a time. Below are some examples of food that are categorised in the different basic tastes — feel free to add different foods to it! If you are going to do all of the basic tastes in one experiment, pick one food from each basic taste to try. If you are going to do one basic taste at a time, then pick two or three foods from that one basic taste.

- Salty: potato chips, roasted seaweed, a dish with lots of salt in it (pasta, chicken wings, kale chips, etc).
- Sweet: ripe banana, milk, biscuits.
- Sour: lemon, sauerkraut, sour lollies.
- Bitter: dark chocolate, Brussels sprouts, olives.

Note: It is important not to hold one basic taste above any other — such as saying bitter is worse than sweet. They may feel that way and that's okay, but the more they try food the more they will love the taste of all of the basic tastes and want to get a mixture of all of the types on their plate.

I remember that when I first had sauerkraut I wasn't a huge fan of the sour taste, but I now love the sour kick to a meal and miss it when it is not there. Same goes for bitter. I grew up thinking bitter foods were lesser foods than sweet foods. Yet most adults love the bitter taste of coffee and chocolate. Seeing Brussels sprouts as bitter yet not in a negative way is a change of awareness for us, yet it is something we can teach our kids as being normal.

Trying time: get your children to try the food and ask where on the tongue they can taste it. Ask them to move it around in their mouths to get it on all parts of their tongue. Mark on the tongue diagram below where they can experience the basic taste, and compare it to where scientists believe those taste buds are on the diagram on page 199. (It can be different — don't say they are wrong, and encourage them to be inquisitive.)

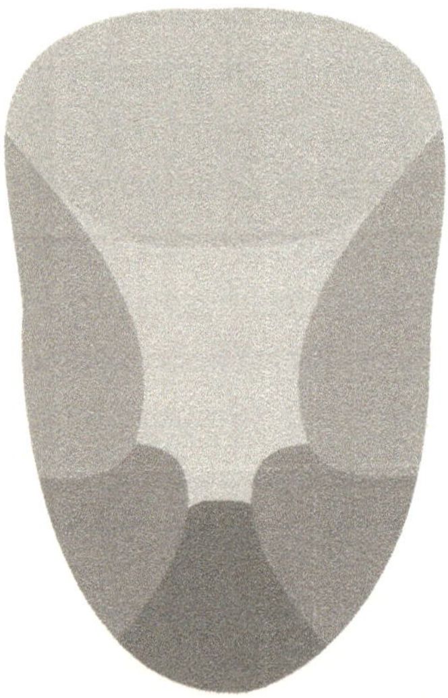

You can repeat these steps for different foods. Or once you get to foodication, you can even ask them if they find the food bitter, sour, salty or sweet.

The more you do this, the more they will have an awareness about foods and their different sensations. If you are starting this with smaller kids, you can guide them a little more, for example: 'This banana is sweet, I can taste it here — where can you taste it?'

ACTION STEPS

1. Go to www.walsnutrition.com/hleresources and print off sheets.
2. Explain and look at the diagram of the tongue and taste buds.
3. Ask if they would like to 'experiment' with the basic tastes.
4. Go through the steps listed above.

Note: It seems that as we age, our taste perception may decrease.[28] Therefore, children may need less of a particular taste to experience it. Also, bitter vegetables can seem a lot more bitter for your children than for you, so if they have a complete aversion to certain foods (broccoli, cabbage, kale, unripe fruits) you may need to leave these foods alone for a bit and come back to them in the future.

CHAPTER ELEVEN

FOODICATION

FOODICATION

Foodication is food education at its best. It is about teaching our children to love real food. It is about getting children to not only be involved in food choices but letting them experiment with and experience food choices themselves. As outlined in the goals on page 196, foodication is not about getting children to like particular foods, it is getting them to develop a positive association with real foods (see page 111 if you are unsure what real foods are). It's about making all food fun.

Step 1: Choose a food to experiment with

Below are drawings of some common vegetables for you to show your children. Ask them what they would like to try. I started with vegetables simply because my children were starting to develop a negative association with vegetables and, let's face it, our society collectively thinks children will not like vegetables. If your children have a real issue with trying new foods, start this process with something you know they do like — fruit, nuts, etc — just make sure it is real food.

Get your children to choose two real foods they want to experiment with. If you have more than one child, ask them all and choose one food for each child. (If you have any cross-overs, great! Go with that food first.) Decide which food you are going to experiment with first.

Step 2: Explore ways to cook/prepare

Once you have your new food, ask what ways your children want to eat it. Below are some traditional ways to cook or prepare vegetables, but encourage your children to come up with their own ways (and do not judge them for it!). In our home, for example, we have vege chanannas, which basically means the vegetable item with cheese and banana on top, i.e. broccoli chanana is a small piece of lightly cooked broccoli with a slice of cheese and a slice of banana on top — down the hatch!

Ways to cook, prepare and serve vegetables:

BOIL

SAUTÉ IN BUTTER AND/OR TAMARI SAUCE

GRATE

ROAST

STEAM

RAW – AS IS

WITH MELTED CHEESE ON TOP

IN A MUFFIN (e.g. ZUCCHINI GRATED INTO A SAVOURY MUFFIN MIX)

DIPPED IN SAUCE OR SPREAD (HUMMUS, COTTAGE CHEESE, etc)

AS PART OF A QUICHE

Encourage your children to come up with their own ways to experience the new food.

Note: Portion size does not matter. Even if they eat only a small amount, the point is to get your children to taste it, and to make the process fun.

I recommend trying one new food per week, cooked seven different ways, or if you find this too much, choose how many days would suit you as a family to do this. The more the better, as it will cement the learning and a positive association with food. However, do develop a system that works for you and your family — even if it is just once a week (that's more than none!). You may decide it is broccoli month and have broccoli a different way each week.

Step 3: Try it — rate it

Now comes the fun part. Follow these steps:

- Get your children to help you to prepare the foodication for the evening (or day). For example, teach them what roasting is and how to roast the vegetable. Show them how taking the broccoli out after one minute or two minutes affects the softness of it. (If you don't have much time, this step is not crucial but it is an added bonus.)
- Draw attention to the look and feel of the cooked vegetable. Talk about how when they roast it, it can get a bit more crunchy than if it was boiled. Get them to smell it. Talk to them about how the smell, sight and feel of foods can all affect the way we perceive them. Ask how they could improve the appearance of it to make it look more appealing for next time.
- Ask them to taste it — get them to swirl it around in their mouths. Draw attention to the texture of the food and where they taste it on their tongue (see Tastication, page 199). Talk about what they like, what they dislike.
- Review: Ask them to rate the food using the chart on page 207. Ask them to comment on how they can make it better for next time, either cooked more or cheese added, for example. The point is for them to realise that you can have the same food a variety of ways. Some they will like instantly, others they won't.

Note: It is important to let your children have their opinions, no matter how weird they might sound to you. Once Huxley said that broccoli tasted too sweet. This is not right in my head, but it was right in hers. Foodication is about experimentation, with no wrongs or rights.

Step 4: Congratulations

High-fives, knuckles: celebrate completing a great foodication. Even if they rated the food as the worst thing they have ever tried, give them a high-five for trying. Make it a positive experience, one they will look forward to doing again, a fun time with their family.

COMMON FOODS TO TRY

The possibilities are endless with foodication, from vegetables and fruits to nuts and seeds, then on to herbs and spices. Here's a list of some common foods to try:

- Fruits: banana, apple, melons, kiwifruit, orange, mandarin, pear, passion fruit.
- Vegetables: broccoli, Brussels sprouts, pumpkin.
- Nuts/Seeds: pumpkin seeds, sesame seeds, cashews, chia seeds, Brazil nuts.
- Spices: turmeric, garam masala, coriander seeds, cumin.
- Herbs: thyme, basil, oregano.

Once your children get more in tune with different foods, you can start combining them. Talk about what foods work well together and how you can bring all the tastes of bitter, sweet, salty and sour into one mouthful. They really will be a 'foodie' in the making!

Once you get started, you can do foodication anywhere. When you eat out, you can ask your children what their dinner tastes like and how they would prepare it better (if they can think of a way!). It doesn't have to be real food when you are out — you can even do it with hot chips. They will start to see chips are made so many ways, and that some places make them better than others. This then gives them the ability to be more confident in choosing foods that taste good and feel good for them, not because it is cool to like some sort of food.

FOODICATION

FOOD: ______________________

DAY	COOKING	RATING	COMMENTS
Monday			
Tuesday			
Wednesday			
Thursday			
Friday			
Saturday			
Sunday			

JUST DO WHAT YOU CAN

Foodication is not meant to be overwhelming for you. I can imagine parents really wanting to educate their children on food but missing the point that it is meant to be *fun*! If it is not fun for you and your children, stop and try again in a month or two. However, chances are if you are finding it fun, your children will, too, so start with making sure this is something you want to do, not because you think you should.

UNEXPECTED BENEFITS

When I first started tastication and foodication with my children, I wasn't too sure where it was going to lead. My main goal was for the kids to develop a positive association with real food — specifically vegetables at that time. What did develop astounded me. Here are a few examples from the very start of my experiment.

The kids started to *play* foodication — they would get the play food we had around and start to pretend-play all the lessons we were having, from training taste buds to what sensations and textures they liked and didn't like about the pretend food, even to ways they could improve that food!

They were more likely to try other foods. I remember two days after starting foodication, Rasmus, who had an aversion to avocado, often saying how yuck it was, asked to try my avocado on toast then even requested a piece of avocado toast himself!

They started to speak differently about vegetables. One of my motivations in developing foodication was because Rasmus started to say 'yuck' to vegetables in general. One night when I was putting him to bed, I lay down while he unwound. As some children will do, he started to whisper and talk to himself about the day and what he had experienced. This night he was talking about vegetables and how you need to try them to like them and how good they could taste. While I don't remember the exact words, I do remember thinking 'whoa, he is downloading all the information about foodication and the positive association with vegetables straight into his developing brain'. It really reinforced to me that we, as parents, need to educate our kids about food, because if we don't society and other children will.

Remember, this was only the start. I am constantly observing different ways in which my children are benefiting from foodication, and you will, too. Please, once you start to do this with your children, get in contact with me and send me your stories about how it has changed your children's views towards food (you can find me at www.walsnutrition.com).

ACTION STEPS

1. Print off sheets from the website www.walsnutrition.com/hleresources for foodication.
2. Explain to your children what you are going to do with them — they can start by drawing their favourite vegetable.
3. Choose a food or a couple of foods to start foodication.
4. Brainstorm ways to cook that food that suits you and them.
5. Buy the food you have decided on.
6. Write down a plan for the week — what food you are using and what ways you will cook it.
7. Get excited each evening about foodication and *do it*!

PART IV

Onwards and Upwards

CHAPTER TWELVE

FULL CIRCLE

We have covered a lot of ground. Time to breathe! We have dealt with a lot of information, from facing your own issues with food to what you can do to make dinner times more peaceful, to real, practical applications. We have talked a lot about changing your mindset from nutrient-orientated to habit-orientated, and about how you can get your children on board. We have got super-practical. Now it is time to come full circle.

It started with you and we will finish with you. After all, you are the parent. Everything in this book, when it comes down to it, is about you, about changing the habitual way you parent around food. And changing habits is not easy.

It is easy to get inspired by these ideas and see the good in them, but in the present moment it is even easier to stay the same. I encourage you to take a step back. Effort is required on your part to create happier mealtimes, to create habits that will lead your children to form a healthy relationship with food — effort that will be rewarded 10 times over, not only for your children but for you. You will come to see that what we have covered in this book will not only create happier mealtimes in your household but healthier toddlers, children and adults.

Many's the time I have read a book and felt inspired to incorporate some of the concepts from it into my life. One month later and I have forgotten what I felt so inspired about and I am back at square one! To stop that happening with the information in this book, in this last chapter I will show you some steps to help you change your habits. This will help you to make long-lasting changes. This is where the practicality of what you have read gets put into action; where the rubber meets the road.

Unless you are going through big life changes, the crux of change is making small alterations that are easy to do and will work for both you and your children. A good diet is one that you don't know you're on. Change things slowly. These small changes will add up to large changes over the longer term.

I am reminded about a professional athlete I once had the pleasure of working with. This English rugby league star was a natural talent. When I met him he had played professional rugby for six years but was still only 23 years old. His body was starting to break down and he was inspired to change his diet. Although he was a professional athlete, he had the diet of an overweight couch potato: one to two litres of Coke a day, fast food three or four times a week, sugary cereal for breakfast. You name it, he ate it.

I started slowly with him and implemented small changes. Once he had mastered a specific habit we would move on to the next one. A year went by and his diet was completely changed: drinking water and having maybe only one Coke every month or so, and takeaways only once a week — and healthier takeaways than he had had previously. He would often talk about how he ate in the past and how easy it was for him to change his habits. I think what it came down to was that small changes were easy to make. If he had tried to never drink Coke again from the start, he would have failed.

I suggest starting with you, but in reality anywhere will do. When a building is demolished, the dynamite is put at the stress points. When these give way, the whole building falls.

It is not by chance that I put dealing with your own issues in chapter one. By facing your issues, your energy changes towards food and the way you parent changes as well. It all falls into place. But if you try to change your parenting without first addressing your own issues, you will still make gains, just more slowly.

I had planned this book for about five years. I thought it was a great concept and the idea of writing it was exciting. Once I started, I was excited about my daily goal of doing 2000 words a day.

When reality rolled around and I had to sit down and actually write it, I had to get up at 4am to get in some quality writing time before the children woke up, so it was easy to make excuses. It was not until Ben got sick of me talking and said, quite bluntly but very spot-on, 'You just gotta do it, Wal. No more talk. Set a date to finish it and give it to me on that date,' that the ball-game changed. I was no longer inspired,

I was frightened. I was going to have to 'walk my talk'. What if I got it wrong? What if I didn't do it right? It was much more comfortable to dream and talk about how I was going to do it than to actually do it.

My point is, don't just start talking about it and reflecting on what your parents said to you and about your issues with food, then do nothing. Don't catch yourself saying 'If you're good, I'll give you chips' and just think 'Oh well, I can't change.' I know you can. Don't dream of change. Start making steps to change.

It's all about starting. Once you start, everything gets easier. The hardest part is just starting.

STEPS TO CHANGE

This section could be a book in itself! But I just want to give you a brief overview of how to put your nutrition knowledge into practice.

There is a lot of talk about nutrition. *A lot*. You should do this. You should to that. You have to change this . . . Easier said than done.

When I was fresh out of university, I had an experience that changed the way I talked about nutrition. I was going through the motions, talking about how you should do this and should change that, to one client. This man was a bit older, well educated and very practical. I was a bit nervous, but I thought I knew everything. I was spouting on about how he should do this, and this was bad for him, etc, when he put up his hand for me to stop — just as Simon Cowell does on *The X Factor*, with just about as much arrogance. He said something I will never forget: 'I know everything you say, but that doesn't help me when I get up in the morning and face the realities of the day.' I knew he was right, but we were not taught how to face this situation at university. I didn't have the knowledge back then to do anything other than what I knew, but this did start me on the path of learning more about habit change and the psychology of change.

I have spent many years since looking into habit change and how we can influence. I have come to the conclusion that it is not about 'talking' nutrition, but more about 'coaching' it. When you want to change a habit, especially a major one, you need to go through this five-step process:

1. prioritise
2. why?
3. make it known
4. plan it
5. review it.

1. Prioritise

Write down every habit that you would like to change. Take a look and pick your number one, your priority — one that you instinctively know you need to change first. Looking through your list, you may notice that you would like a few things to change, but just by changing one, the priority of the others will fall into place as well.

Make this very specific. Ask yourself, on a scale of 1–10, can you commit to changing this habit for the next 30 days, with 1 being 'definitely not' and 10 being 'absolutely yes'? If your answer is anything less than a nine, then choose the next priority. If the answer is yes, move on to the next step. If your answer is less than a nine, then choose a habit that you can give a nine — either a smaller step, for example, not never drinking Coke again, but only drinking it on the weekends. Also, think about adding things in rather than taking things out. Instead of saying 'I will not eat any cake', say 'I will eat 10 servings of vegetables a day'. A positive goal is often easier to reach than a restrictive one.

2. Why?

This is an important step. You have read why I think it is important for you to change your habits around food; now it is your chance to ask yourself why it is important for you, and for your children. Maybe you have been through a tough time with food and you can see your children heading in the same direction and you are scared of that, or maybe you just want something more for your children. Why does changing mean so much to you?

Hint: The more emotions you bring up about this, the more likely you are to keep it at the forefront of your mind on a daily basis.

3. Make it known

Write down what you want to change and discuss how you want to change things with your partner or someone close. Stick it up on your fridge. Put it in your pocket if you must, and rub it when you need an extra boost of encouragement. Just get it out in the open.

4. Plan it

This step is arguably the most crucial. Have you ever said 'I am never drinking again' when you were nursing a hangover? But the next time someone offers you a wine to finish that oh-so-long day you forget about the words you spoke and you down that wine!

You need to plan. Think about all the situations you will be in which may lead you to not follow through on your new habit. Devise ways to encourage yourself to pause and follow through.

Only you will know what situations will arise for you. The more you plan, the higher your chances will be to create a habit.

5. Review it

Do a brief debrief every day — when you were awesome, where you could improve, and how. Most of all, congratulate yourself. We are so quick to judge ourselves when we don't get it right, but when we have a little win we forget to congratulate ourselves. Make sure you congratulate yourself, as this will help you get through the next day.

ACTION STEPS

1. Go through these five steps. Do it now.
2. Write one change you will make, and commit to it.

HABITS ARE HABITS, NOT RULES

I have created a general habit in both myself and my children of eating dinner as our last meal of the day. However, once Ben and I decided to tackle the three-hour drive from my parents' home to my in-laws' at night. The plan was that the children would fall asleep early on in the drive and we would have a great chat.

We set off at 7pm, after dinner. One hour down we were driving past a city where we decided to stop. The plan was not going that well; all three children were still wide awake. 'I'm hungry,' Huxley said, so we decided to stop at a supermarket so they could run around and we could get something to eat.

Now this goes against two habits I have outlined: eating after dinner and snacking on the go. Can you guess why I would be okay with it on this occasion? For one, a habit is just that: a habit. I am guessing you, like most people, have a habit of brushing your teeth before bed. Yet I am sure you can think of at least one night you went to bed with furry teeth because you were not in your normal situation. Travelling in the car after dinner was an unusual circumstance. Also, Huxley only asks for something to eat after dinner on the odd occasion. It has become her habit to not eat after dinner. When she does ask for something it is because she is hungry and I believe her. Whatever the reason, I trust that she knows her own body. If I thought of the habits like rules I would be rigid in my parenting, ultimately not fostering autonomy and a healthy relationship with food in Huxley.

THE BIGGER PICTURE

Often we get so narrow-minded in what we think is the right way to do things that we forget what we are trying to achieve. By concentrating on getting little Johnny to eat his beans we have forgotten that it is not really about the beans, but about keeping him healthy and happy.

One day I watched Huxley and Rasmus in the bath together. They had an impending game of Uno to play and they wanted to quickly clean themselves, get dry and into their bedtime clothes to sit down for the game. When they got in the bath, they got so fixated on who was going to use the soap first that they forgot why they wanted to use the soap.

It was a stand-off, and they took such a long time arguing about who was going to use it first, each not wanting to give in, that it ate into their Uno time. It wasn't about the soap at all, it was about getting clean quickly. If one had realised this, they both could have been out of the bath in a quarter of the time it took them that day. They were fixated on the short term — 'who is using the soap first?' — not the long-term — 'get clean quick for a game of Uno'.

Continually remind yourself that this is long-term stuff. It is not about eating the beans but the habits you are creating. This gives you space to breathe in those situations where your children seem to be as stubborn as mules. When you have no vested interest in the specific outcome of eating beans, you can parent with more control of your reactions, in more of a coaching way. Your frustrations are lessened. You have a better ability to respond to your child's needs. As a consequence, you create happy memories. After all, is that not what parenting is all about? Creating happy memories?

If you are anything like me, you will want to practise everything that you learn in this book. Just the mere fact that you have this book in your hands means you are a reflective parent and want more for your children than you currently know. You want to know and practise everything *now*.

My advice is, give yourself room to improve. It's okay to make mistakes. This is how we learn: through doing, through experience.

When you try to get the big stuff right, you forget about the little stuff. When you worry whether your children are healthy enough, you can get into a routine of forcing, controlling, bribing and coercing your children into eating how you want them to eat. You forget it is about connecting with your children.

When you give up on those elusive ideals of what you expect your children and yourself to be, your parenting completely changes. The irony is that children seem to relax more and become what we were trying to force them to be! My bond, in general, with my children has strengthened — all because I started to think about habits, about the long-term picture of food and how it affects my children. You can bond over food experiences rather than fight.

At some stage you may also start to feel overwhelmed. You will realise just how many words you say to your children that may not be instilling a belief you want. Whenever I get overwhelmed with anything in my life, I sit down and narrow my focus. Do one thing and do it well (and go through steps to change that habit). Put all your energy into that one thing and forget about the rest.

You may decide to start with yourself first, to change some things you do around food. You may start with simply talking about checking-in. Just narrow your focus and start. You will soon realise that it gets easier and easier.

I care. I care about you. I encourage you to keep learning, reflecting and striving to be the best parent you can be for your children. Realise that parenting is a journey, a growth experience for you as much as it is for your children.

I am excited about you starting your journey.

FREQUENTLY ASKED QUESTIONS

I often get asked similar questions during talks and when working with clients. Below are the answers to the questions which are most frequently asked.

1. CAN I SERVE DESSERT?

A lot of parents ask me this. My answer is 'Yes, if you like.' After all, it is not about the 'what' but the 'how'. 'How' you serve dessert is what the question should be. 'How' depends on what you are comfortable with. You can either serve dessert with dinner alongside the spinach, or you can serve it, as typically served, after dinner (see page 173 for more on this). If you serve it with dinner you can prompt your children to take a bit of everything. If you think this is too much for your children, then serve it afterwards. But instead of saying 'Finish all your spinach and you will get dessert', keep asking about checking-in and then say, 'Make sure you leave some room for dessert'.

Only your children can really know their hunger cues. It is up to us to guide them and trust them. If you really don't think they have had enough to eat of their dinner, then keep their dinner out and offer it to them after the dessert if they say they are still hungry.

2. IF YOU DON'T BELIEVE IN LABELLING FOODS GOOD OR BAD, WHY IS IT NOT A FREE-FOR-ALL?

You need to provide your children with guidelines. They do not have the ability to realise what is good for them and what is not so good. It takes time to comprehend and make connections that some foods leave us feeling great while others do not.

By letting children have as much sugar and fried food as they like, they can form an addiction of sorts to this food.[29] This messes with internal hunger cues.

Having a healthy relationship with food is a learnt skill. Just like learning to cross the road is taught in stages depending on the age and comprehension level of the child, so is the skill of eating. At the start they need more guidance. When we first start solids with our babies, we don't expect them to know how to hold a knife and fork and feed themselves. They gradually build up to eating with a knife and fork.

It's the same with food choices. When our babies start solids we are not asking them what they want to eat — they have never tried any of it before, so how could they know? But over the course of 18 years or so we are teaching our children about food. It needs to be a gradual learning, not 'Okay, now you know how to walk, here's the road to practise on!'

Free-for-all will come at some stage, no doubt. For now it is about giving them boundaries, and teaching them *why* there are boundaries will help your children to develop a healthy relationship with food that will take them into their adult years.

3. MY CHILD SEEMS TO CRAVE SWEETS AND FRIED FOOD, AND OFTEN SNEAKS THEM. WHY IS THIS?

First of all, is this a reflection of your behaviour? Do you sneak food? Can you be totally honest with yourself, your children and strangers about your food intake without feeling guilty? Secondly, talk to them. Ask them why. When they say they want to eat lollies all day every day, don't judge. Listen to what they are saying, then tell them how you know that eating lollies is not so good for them, and that you love them and want the best for them. Ask if you can meet them halfway: you can have lollies but only after you have some real food.

I encourage you to experiment. What food creates satisfaction in your children the longest? You can use the 'start the day right experiment' sheet (see page 232), not just for the start of the day but for any meal. Growing children need more fat than we do as adults. Therefore give them avocado, full-fat Greek yoghurt, cheese, nuts. See if this can help them satisfy their hunger and cure their habit of sneaking food.

4. MY CHILD DOESN'T EAT AT ALL. NOT EVEN SWEET FOOD. I AM JUST HAPPY WHEN SHE EATS ANYTHING. WHAT CAN I DO?

Again, look to yourself. Are your children picking up on your issues, or are you putting too many expectations on them, not just with food but in life in general? Some children respond to pressure by shutting down. Not eating is a way for them to exert control over some aspect of their lives, as it can be the only aspect they can control. If you relax, do they follow suit and eat more?

Secondly, remember it is about habits. Providing your children with processed food all day is not going to help them long term. Be open and honest with them. Open up a dialogue with them about how you are concerned that they are not eating enough to meet their growth needs. Ask if they ever feel hungry, where they feel it, what satisfies them. Also, keep healthy snack food convenient. The more they see it, the more likely they are to just take one or two bites (for example, having vegetable sticks available pre-dinner).

5. MY CHILD HAS BEEN IN A TRAUMATIC SITUATION AND HAS STOPPED EATING. WHAT CAN I DO?

You will need to see an expert and get individualised advice, and I encourage any parent or caregiver to do this if their child is suffering from some food issue as a result of a traumatic situation in their life.

However, that doesn't mean that the ideas presented in this book cannot help you outside of expert help. If they have stopped eating or are eating very little and only what they like, if you reward or be restrictive in their diet to help them eat more of a variety you will probably find they will dig their toes in more. As I mentioned above, food is one area of their lives which children can control, and when they have been in a traumatic situation and feel out of control in their lives they are not going to give this control up easily.

What is important here is to be empathetic, and above all do not label them. If they hear you telling other parents, family and friends about how they won't eat, they will live up to this label even though they may be healing emotionally from the traumatic situation. So just make sure you keep an awareness about food and do not label them as a bad eater.

6. MY CHILD SEEMS TO BE ALWAYS HUNGRY DURING THE DAY, BUT THEN WON'T EAT HIS DINNER. WHAT CAN I DO?

When children snack all day on processed food and limited real food, parents worry more about them eating dinner. Dinner becomes the only chance they have to get real food into their children. However, when you make snacking on real food first a habit, not eating at dinner times becomes a non-issue.

Having consistent mealtimes and snack-eating times works well here. Work out times when you will give your children snacks and meals. Enlist their help to work out when they feel hunger the most, like after school. When they come to you outside of these times saying they are hungry, you can reply, 'Good, you only have half an hour until snack time. Would you like _____ or _____?' Letting them be hungry for a short period will not hurt them and, if anything, teaches them the capacity to deal with hunger.

Also, keep in mind that children do have growth spurts at times. When they do, they tend to be hungrier than normal. Make sure they are filling up on real food and now-and-again food to help their bodies grow strong.

7. THIS IS ALL SO OVERWHELMING. I CAN'T REMEMBER TO DO EVERYTHING HERE, SO WHERE SHOULD I START?

I know this can be very overwhelming. It was for me at first, especially because I could see that what I was doing was not in line with encouraging my children to have a healthy relationship with food and I really wanted the best for my children. But when we get overwhelmed, it is negating the information in this book. Just start with one meal and one encouragement. As most parents struggle with the evening meal, just start with trying new foods at dinner.

It may even start with you first. Pick out a vegetable that you don't normally buy and cook with that. You can make it as an option for your children or just keep it on your own plate, but draw their attention to it, saying how you want to train your taste buds to try new and different food.

There are no right or wrong places to start, with one meal or another, with one habit or even starting with yourself. Small increments will add up; the important thing is just starting somewhere.

8. MY CHILDREN HAVE AN AVERSION TO ANYTHING AND EVERYTHING NEW — THERE IS NO WAY THEY WILL TRY ANY NEW FOOD. WHAT SHOULD I DO?

For some children, trying anything new, whether it's food or activities, can be completely overwhelming. As I have already mentioned, for some children trying new food may start with trying other new things . . . nothing to do with food. Trying new things is like a muscle; the more you exercise it, the more it becomes stronger. But be gentle.

Another thing you can do to introduce something new to your kids is make it not new. Often when we have our first child and they go off to kindergarten or school it can be very overwhelming for them and they can (literally) kick up a fuss about going. Fast-forward to your third child and they go off to school happily. What is the difference?

The first child was often just chucked into the new situation. They had only been to a school or day-care once or twice — sometimes it's the first time they have seen it — yet their parents are leaving them there. What the . . .? However, the third has been to the same school or kindergarten the older one has gone to many times before, to pick up their siblings. To them it is not new, and they know one day they will get to go there.

If your child has an aversion to anything new, get them comfortable with it first. Talk about all the fun times and great things they will see and do. Also, with food talk about how you don't want them to miss out on all the delicious foods they could have just because they don't want to try. Read the children's book *Huxley the Duckling* (written for Huxley by Ben, and available through Amazon), which is about trying something new and the adventures that ensue. Keep giving your child this message — they will get it sooner or later that trying new things is not only good but can be fun!

9. MY CHILD DOES NOT EVEN SIT AT THE TABLE DURING OUR EVENING MEAL. WE TRY BUT IT ENDS UP A BATTLE OF WILLS RATHER THAN A PEACEFUL DINNER TIME. WHAT CAN WE DO?

Children will do this for a variety of reasons. Firstly, it may be their way of asserting control. I know you really want a happy dinner time, so let him/her go. Tell them that you would love them to join you at the dinner table but are happy to let them play but not around the dinner table. Then make the dinner time as happy as it can be. It may take a while but sooner or later they will want to join in!

Also, make sure they are hungry for dinner. If they are snacking right up to dinner time they may be so full that they don't want any more food. Developing set eating times can help to eliminate this. Setting a certain time at which they have their last snack — say an hour and a half before you have dinner — can be a way to make sure they are hungry for dinner yet not so out of energy they are throwing tantrums left, right and centre. Also, keeping the time you serve dinner and the pre-dinner snack constant can help them with knowing what times they should expect food.

10. CAN I TAKE MY CHILDREN OUT TO DINNER WHILE TEACHING THEM ABOUT FOOD?

Absolutely. In fact, I could argue that it is beneficial for them. When going out to dinner, especially when they are encountering different cuisines, you can make it a really fun experience to try new foods — you may be trying new foods as well, which adds to their experience when they see how you react to new foods. You can talk to them about how children in that different culture grow up eating that food and how if they were from there they would be eating ______ and ______. (Tip: If you make it something that sounds yucky, they are likely to laugh and it will be a real eye-opener up for them.)

You could even have a family habit that whenever you go out for dinner they (and you) need to have at least one bit of something new, taking turns to choose that new food. Make it fun!

11. AT WHAT AGE CAN I START THIS WITH MY CHILDREN?

This book is primarily written for two- to seven-year-olds, yet the concepts in this book are just as relevant for older children, and even adults.

From my experience, I think reading this book *before* you have children could save *a lot* of issues. It is easier to form a habit than break one.

I was listening to a parenting podcast one day and the hosts were talking about screen-time and how to limit that in their children. Specifically, they started to talk about screen-time before school and putting strategies in place to limit this, such as having to get everything ready first, etc.

I got thinking about this, as my children do not have a problem with screen-time before school — not because they are perfect, but because TV/iPads, etc have *never* been on before school. They never ask or never watch anything because they do not have a habit of doing it. I didn't do this intentionally, but it made me think. It is so much easier to implement something like a habit of not having screen-time before school than trying to break that habit later on.

Certainly, reading this book before you start giving your children solids will help you to decide which habits you want your kids to have and to teach them from day one. I have done this with my third child, Eckhart. Although it is harder to encourage toddlers to eat something like sauerkraut, if you are having it, they want to have it as well.

Eckhart in some ways is a much more adventurous eater than my older two. She even loves to eat spicy hot curries, which is something I inadvertently told my other two children when they were younger that they would not like. Guess what? They still don't love curry, although Huxley, the oldest, is slowly coming around.

12. I FIND FOODICATION AND TASTICATION TAKES TOO MUCH TIME AND EFFORT — IS THERE ANOTHER WAY?

Sure, there are plenty of ways to teach our children about food — in fact, send me some of your ideas, I would love to hear them. However, I guess if you are asking for a quick fix or something that requires little effort, then I am going to say no. As I have mentioned plenty of times, teaching our children about food is a skill, and skills are mastered over a period of time. I guess what it comes down to is priorities. For myself, nutrition is one of the biggest priorities in my parenting. It might not be everyone's, but it is mine. And whatever we think is the priority for our children we will put the most effort into.

Teaching children about food through the foodication and tastication system does require some planning, yet the pay-off (your children's positive relationship with food) is *huge*. Not only does it go a long way to making sure they are leading a healthy life, but they will also have fewer issues with food. Their energy won't be taken up with guilt, struggles with willpower and all those emotions that often come with food, which means they will have more energy for other aspects of their life.

Whenever putting time and energy into a project, I always ask myself why; what emotional reasons do I have for doing this? Putting emotions into the reason why is enough to spring some people into action. I know it was for me.

13. WHILE I LIKE SOME OF THE CONCEPTS IN THIS BOOK, I FIND SOME OF YOUR SUGGESTIONS TOO MUCH FOR MY CHILDREN TO HANDLE. WHAT SHOULD I DO?

This book was designed, in a way, like a blueprint. If you can understand the concept, especially in the first half of the book, you are halfway there already. No two children are the same, so I don't think all the suggestions in this book will be your magic answer. If you have mastered the blueprint, I know you will come up with unique ways to teach your kids, especially about having a healthy relationship with food.

THE BLUEPRINT

1. Awareness — about your beliefs and society's beliefs around food and being able to challenge them not as set in stone but as just a belief.
2. Your parenting style — seeing that coaching your children has more favourable outcomes than other parenting styles when teaching kids to develop a healthy relationship with food.
3. Seeing the development of a relationship with food as a skill to be learnt. Food skills are habits, habits you will choose knowingly or unknowingly. You choose what habits to instil and then think about how to break down teaching those habits on a daily basis.
4. It's never too late. It is never too late to encourage your children or yourself to form a healthy relationship with food — after all, it is just a habit and you can break and form habits!

APPENDIX

START THE DAY RIGHT EXPERIMENT

DATE:

EXPERIMENT: To find out what type of breakfast energises me.

TIME OF BREAKFAST:

WHAT I HAD TO EAT (WITH APPROXIMATE PORTION SIZES): Do this for three different types of breakfast meals (e.g. porridge, eggs with avocado, etc) and repeat each twice.

TIME I GOT HUNGRY AGAIN:

HOW I FELT: Happy Sad Angry Excited Irritable

DID I FEEL BLOATED? (describe to compare for next time)

MY ENERGY LEVELS (0 = LOW, 10 = SUPER ENERGETIC):

ENDNOTES

1. Bruce Lipton, author of *Biology of Belief*, Hay House, 2008, has amazing insights on subconscious and conscious habitual thoughts. This online article is an interesting read: www.brucelipton.com/resource/article/happy-healthy-child-holistic-approach (retrieved 17 November 2015).

2. For the privacy of others I have not used real names in this book.

3. Read Dr Joe Dispenza's books for more information about brain-forming habits, or read this online article: www.drjoedispenza.com/index.php?page_id=the_waves_of_future (retrieved 17 November 2015).

4. Brian Wansink PhD is a powerhouse of information on this topic. He has published many articles and books on eating behaviour, including the bestseller *Mindless Eating: Why We Eat More Than We Think*, Bantam, New York, 2010, and *Slim by Design: Mindless Eating Solutions for Everyday Life*, William Morrow, New York, 2013.

5. S. Scaglioni, C. Arizza, F. Vecchi and S. Tedeschi, 'Determinants of children's eating behavior', *American Journal of Clinical Nutrition*, December 2011, 94 (6 Suppl.) 2006s–2011s.

6. Sylvie Issanchou and Sophie Nicklaus, *Sensitive Periods and Factors in the Early Formation of Food Preferences*. Retrieved from http://ebook.ecog-obesity.eu/chapter-nutrition-food-choices-eating-behavior/sensitive-periods-factors-early-formation-food-preferences/ (retrieved 17 November 2015).

7. E. Haycraft and J. Blissett, 'Controlling feeding practices and psychopathology in a non-clinical sample of mothers and fathers', *Eating Behaviours*, 2008, 9 (4), pp. 484–92.

8. Ruchika Talwar, Janet D. Carter and David H. Gleaves, 'New Zealand female body image: what roles do ethnicity and body mass play?' Retrieved from www.psychology.org.nz/wp-content/uploads/Talwar1.pdf (retrieved 17 November 2015).

9. Baumrind suggested that the majority of parents display one of three different parenting styles. Further research by Maccoby and Martin also suggested the addition of a fourth parenting style. See D. Baumrind, 'Effects of authoritative parental control on child behaviour', *Child Development*, 1966, 37 (4), pp. 887–907.

10. Fisher and Birch are some of the top researchers in the area of parental food control. See articles such as: J. O. Fisher and L. L. Birch, 'Restricting access to palatable foods affects children's behavioural response, food selection, and intake', *American Journal of Clinical Nutrition*, 1999, 69, pp. 1264–72 and J. O. Fisher and L. L. Birch, 'Restricting access to food and children's eating', *Appetite*, 1999, 32, pp. 405–19.

11. L. L. Birch and D. W. Marlin, 'I don't like it; I never tried it: effects of exposure on 2-year-old children's food preferences', *Appetite: Journal for Intake Research*, 1982, 3, pp. 353–60.

12. Ibid.

13. See Fisher and Birch, endnote 10.

14. S. Worchel, J. Lee and A. Adewole, 'Effects of supply and demand on ratings of object value', *Journal of Personality and Social Psychology*, 1975, 32, 906–14.

15. There is an excellent blog post by Kiyah Duffey PhD titled 'Food on the brain: how advertising can influence your child's diet' on Dr Dave Walsh's website. Retrieved from http://drdavewalsh.com/posts/166 (retrieved January 2015).

16. J. B. Furness, W. A. Kunze and N. Clerc, 'Nutrient tasting and signaling mechanisms in the gut. II. The intestine as a sensory organ: neural, endocrine, and immune responses', *American Journal of Physiology*, 1999, 277(5 Pt 1):G922–8.

17. Brian Wansink, *Mindless Eating: Why We Eat More Than We Think*, Bantam, New York, 2010.

18. Ben has written a children's book. *Huxley the Duckling* is on Amazon and is a story about how trying new foods can lead to exciting adventures.

19. S. P. Kremers, J. Brug, H. de Vries and R. C. Engles, 'Parenting style and adolescent fruit consumption', *Appetite*, August 2003, 41(1), pp. 43–50.

20. C. Caldwell and S. Hibbet, 'Play that one again: the effect of music tempo on consumer behaviour in a restaurant' (abstract) www.acrwebsite.org/search/view-conference-proceedings.aspx?Id=11116 (retrieved February 2015).

21. Brian Wansink, *Slim by Design: Mindless Eating Solutions for Everyday Life*, William Morrow, New York, 2013.

22. Brian Wansink, Koert van Ittersum and James M. Painter, 'How descriptive food names bias sensory perceptions in restaurants', *Food Quality and Preference*, 2005, 16, pp. 393–400.

23. Ibid.

24. I make these myself and it is very easy. Take seeds and sprinkle over Bragg liquid aminos, found at most supermarkets, or tamari sauce. Bake at 150°C until just browned (15–20 minutes), turning once or twice while cooking.

25. Definition from www.dictionary.com.

26. Dr Wayne W. Dyer has written several amazing books. The one referred to with memes is *Change Your Thoughts — Change Your Life*, Hay House, Carlsbad, CA, 2007.

27. Harvey Karp, author of *The Happiest Toddler on the Block: How to Eliminate Tantrums and Raise a Patient, Respectful, and Cooperative One- to Four-Year-Old*, Bantam, New York, 2008, has also written *The Happiest Baby on the Block: The New Way to Calm Crying and Help Your Newborn Sleep Better*, Bantam, New York, 2003 — a good read for parents.

28. J. M. Boyce and G. R. Shone, 'Effects of ageing on smell and taste', *Postgraduate Medical Journal*, 2006, 82 (966) 239–41. Retrieved from http://www.ncbi.nlm.nih.gov/pmc/articles/PMC2579627/ (retrieved 17 November 2015)

29. Ashley N. Gearhardt, Sonja Yokum, Patrick T. Orr, Eric Stice, William R. Corbin and Kelly D. Brownell, 'Neural correlates of food addiction', *Archives of General Psychiatry*, 2011, 68(8), pp. 808–16.

INDEX

RANDOM HOUSE

UK | USA | Canada | Ireland | Australia
India | New Zealand | South Africa | China

Random House is an imprint of the Penguin Random House group of companies, whose addresses can be found at global.penguinrandomhouse.com.

Penguin Random House New Zealand

First published by Penguin Random House New Zealand, 2016

1 3 5 7 9 10 8 6 4 2

The information and advice given in this book is general in nature and should not be treated as personalised professional advice. Should you or a member of your family have specific dietary needs or problems such as allergies, please consult a health professional.

Cover and text design by Kate Barraclough © Penguin Random House New Zealand
Illustrations on pages 94 and 203 by Sam Bunny
Cover photograph © JW LTD/Getty Images
Printed and bound in Australia by Griffin Press, an Accredited ISO AS/NZS 14001 Environmental Management Systems Printer

A catalogue record for this book is available from the National Library of New Zealand.

ISBN 978-1-77553-864-6
eISBN 978-1-77553-866-0

penguinrandomhouse.co.nz

MIX
Paper from responsible sources
FSC® C009448